WITH HEART
AND MIND

WITH HEART AND MIND

BY RICHARD TAYLOR

ST. MARTIN'S PRESS • NEW YORK

A version of *"De Anima"* has appeared in *The American Philosophical Quarterly*, Vol. 10, January, 1973, and a version of "Perishing" appears in the revised edition of my *Metaphysics* under the title "Being and Nothing," Prentice-Hall, Inc., 1973. Both are included in this collection with permission.

Copyright © 1973 by Richard Taylor
All rights reserved. For information, write:
St. Martin's Press, Inc., 175 Fifth Ave., New York, N.Y. 10010.
Manufactured in the United States of America
Library of Congress Catalog Card Number: 72-96436

AFFILIATED PUBLISHERS: Macmillan Limited, London
—also at Bombay, Calcutta, Madras and Melbourne

For Hylda,
who gave me eyes to see with

PROEM

These thoughts, although of a philosophical character, contain no philosophical dialectic. They seek instead to convey a certain vision and so might appropriately be called a collage or a montage, were such words not pretentious. Let us simply say they are a picture.

The picture, if one were to try encapsulating it into a few words, is probably the oldest philosophical and religious idea known to man: That being is one and identical with God the creator. Exactly the same picture is rediscovered in every age and in every corner of the world. It is at once terrifying and completely fulfilling. It will never perish, and nothing will ever finally replace it. Nothing possibly can; its endurance is that of the stars. Wise men, seers, philosophers, prophets, poets, hymnists, mystics, try again and again to paint this picture, in parable, declamation, psalm, poem, fable, dialectic, allegory and song, and I have added my own small effort. I have tried to express in various ways, some grave and some lighthearted, and some whimsical, what it is like to see at last, to penetrate the illusions that encompass us, to be in a certain state of heart and mind that can only be described, however prosaically, as an absolute love for God and the world, a love that banishes all arising and perishing, and reveals an identity of every spirit to the rest of a creation that is precious beyond any possibility of utterance.

CONTENTS

WITH HEART AND MIND • 1
FOUR STEPS • 6
LOVE AND SEPARATION • 8
EMPIRICISM • 12
LONELINESS • 17
EGOISM • 18
THE ETERNAL • 23
ALIENATION • 27
SELF-LOVE • 31
DIVINE LOVE • 35
MONISM • 39
ARISING • 44
PERISHING • 46
THE ILLUSION OF SELFHOOD • 55
THE FULLNESS OF GOD • 61
A BEGINNING • 67
THE MYSTIC • 70
SEDUCTIVE LOVE • 73

... AND MIND • 76
"WHEN I WAS A CHILD ..." • 77
TRUE LOVE • 79
THE VISIBLE CHURCH • 80
NATURA NATURANS • 82
NOT TRYING • 84
PLATONIC LOVE • 85
SUNDAY • 88
PHILOSOPHICAL LOVE • 90
LOVE AND FULFILLMENT • 93
THE ANGELS • 98
PARADOXES OF PAIN • 99
EVERYTHING ELSE • 106
SEEKERS • 108
MANY AND ONE • 116
CARTESIAN FLIMFLAM • 119
DE ANIMA • 122
A SURROGATE OF LOVE • 134
THE INDESTRUCTIBLE EGO • 136
APPEARANCES AND REALITY • 140
DOING AND BEING • 144
EPHEMERAE • 146

WITH HEART
AND MIND

WITH HEART AND MIND

We are continuously assailed by two voices. One gives the testimony of the intellect or reason, the other that of simply seeing; and while one might suppose that the two would coincide, they seldom do. In fact they tend to say opposite things. Men generally heeded the latter and felt at home in the world, until they invented philosophy and science. Since then, reason has been elevated to the role of judge over all, even over matters on which it has absolutely nothing to say. In such cases its judgment is simply to silence the voice of vision. If, for example, we proclaim our love for God, responding to the voices heeded by our distant ancestors, before anyone had ever heard of philosophy, then the voice of intellect declares this to be a rationally groundless fiction. If the spirit of our living discloses itself in the stars far away and the sands beneath our feet, intellect declares this, too, to be poetry and feeling, empty of truth.

Of course what is allowable by the intellect usually turns out to be dead right, sooner or later. It is obviously right, to anyone who looks at things in that light. It is a great blunder to try to show that the rational apprehension of things is mistaken; to try to *show,* for example, that we are God's children. Any rational conception has already been subjected to the most rigorous testing; it is not now suddenly going to fail one of *our* tests.

But strangely, we eventually discover that when we say the very opposite of what is allowable by fastidious reason, the very opposite of what intelligence declares to be so, we sometimes are still saying what is true, sometimes resoundingly so. The discovery of this tends to turn one against his own reason, and he is likely to be thought of as a lover of darkness and a mystic. Still, we should not be so taken in by the confident posturing of intelligence that we fail to note that reason can be an incredible ass.

Intelligence, in keeping with its intense concern for hard fact, informs me that I am a being of almost total insignificance. A short while ago—a moment ago, in the context of that eternity over which the stars preside—I was deposited in the world with an immeasurable casualness, with no more concern than is bestowed upon the birth of a bacterium. At the moment my existence began in conception, had a minute particle veered ever so slightly in any of infinitely many possible ways, then I would never have existed at all. Another would have existed in my place, perhaps (perhaps not), but it would not have been me, would not have been the unique self I find myself to be. And had a similar tiny particle swerved ever so slightly at the moment my father's existence began, then he would never have been—nor I, inasmuch as I sprang from him. The same may be said for that moment when my mother's existence began. And the same for every one of my ancestors, back into the remotest reaches of time. At each of those moments, at each of those countless moments, there was one chance in a million that a given event would take place, an event upon which my own eventual existence absolutely depended. It cannot then be imagined that it ever really mattered whether I should exist. That one great event, great to me but a zero to the rest of the world, that event which was the very first beginning of my particular, unique existence—that event had, throughout the numberless ages before it happened, an infinitesimally small chance of happening at all.

It cannot, therefore, be of any importance that I am, except of course to me. But my caring that something should be so, does not make it the least important that it is so, except, again, to me.

And as I came into being a short while ago, as a consequence of the most improbable concatenation of coincidences over ages and ages of time, so in a short while I shall cease to exist; and this cessation has an inevitability as absolute as was the improbability that I would ever exist in the first place. My eyes will open for the last time; my heart will beat for the one last time; I shall taste my last drop forever; and the loves and hates, pain and rejoicing, all that belonged to my life, will be effaced once and for all, as though they had never been. The rest of the world, all that is *not* me, will go on, perhaps endlessly, but without me, and it will very shortly be as though I had never existed at all, my existence then mattering as little as that of a housefly.

It is a dreary picture, set forth by reason and intelligence, and it is natural to bring to mind, for comparison, such images as that of an insect enjoying a moment of sunlight, then falling to mingle again with the sand for another eternity. But it is also the voice of intellect which notes that truth was never guaranteed to fortify one's conceits, pride and selfishness.

Now, however, my heart, mind and vision kindle a fire where I would have least expected it. Pretty much expecting some declaration that the foregoing picture really is not so —that I, as a person, as a soul perhaps, as a special creation of God perhaps, am a being of dignity, or of conscience, or of supreme worth—I am flabbergasted to find the testimony of vision demolishing my significance even more completely than did that of my reason. For this angel of vision declares: There is no self, no ego, no soul, no I, no thou, no mine, no thine! These are but words, springing from illusion and marking no real distinctions at all. What is real is not a minute self that contemplates the rest of reality as a spectator, more or less removed. That spectator does not exist. What is real is nature, ever changing, ever creating, in response to no will but its own. That reality is ungenerable and indestructible. It is no creation of God, except as God creates Himself. You do not exist as a sojourner in that world, as a being who arrives there, whether by chance or otherwise, and then eventually departs. You exist as that very nature itself, inseparable from it, for it alone is real. To nothing can you point and say: This is my self, this is me, this is my ego, my true being. And just as little can you point to anything and say: That is other, that is not me, not myself.

Yet strangely, to whatever you point, you can in truth say: This *is* myself, this is me, this is my ego, my true being. And you cannot possibly be wrong, no matter where you happen to be pointing.

FOUR STEPS

We can discern four stages in the development of the spirit. Most men seem forever imprisoned in the first, though certainly not without intimations of the others. They are stages from isolation and loneliness, at the one extreme, to the perception of identity and the love of God, at the other, and they can be superficially characterized as:

1. Egoism: The awareness of oneself as distinct and as that to which all of heaven and earth are presented.
2. Nihilism: The abortive effort of self-denial through sheer negation and response to the demands of duty.
3. Love: Self-denial through the affirmation of life, and the replacement of duty to others with the perception of identity.
4. Salvation: The transcendence of the self through the perception of oneself as belonging in God the creator.

There is no clear, straightforward way of describing any of these, nor is there anything fixed or magical in the number four—it could have been six, eight or a dozen. But we can, from various angles, characterize the various levels at which existence is possible. Doubtless they are usually quite mixed up together and, while mutually exclusive conceptually, they are not existentially so in the least. Perhaps it is even a redeeming quality in a holy man that he is still a man and therefore still capable of utter childishness.

LOVE AND SEPARATION

Love is a perception of identity. It is only by such a perception that the distinction between the *me* and the *thee* is abolished. The abolishment of this distinction is not merely the necessary condition of loving; it is just what loving is. All those other relationships that men have called loving—cooperating, giving and taking, possessing and, most remarkably of all, copulating—only superficially resemble loving, in one way or another. They at first glance *appear* to be states wherein the interpersonal gulf is bridged, though in fact it is as absolute as ever.

So long as I think of myself as an absolute, so long as, like Descartes, I think of myself as something existing in my own right, ultimately distinct from everything else, then there is only one possible way I can view the rest, and that is as *other,* as something alien. In the presence of this other, which carries with it the possibility of threat to what I think of as mine, my natural response is to withdraw into my shell, into an acknowledged separateness and abandonment.

Lovelessness is thus the perception of difference, of a gulf between me and thee across which we can only communicate, in the sense of sending (or rather offering) and receiving (or acknowledging) messages. From my point of view, which is that of a center of existence, such communication is only a tenuous interaction, very liable to failure, between me, the central existence, and the other, or that which is peripheral. Only with the abolishment of that gulf can there be communication in its true and original sense of "giving to another as partaker" (Oxford Univ. Dict.).

It is not being suggested that men should pretend not to notice their differences, that they should try to act as though these did not exist, and that they should baptize these attitudes as "love." This is indeed a common conception of love, and one that we are constantly exhorted to cultivate. In no other way could love ever have been represented as a *duty,* as it frequently is. Kant even made this a pivotal point of his ethics. But clearly, I can think of it as a duty to love others only if I do regard them as *other.* It would be silly to speak of my having a duty to love that with which I entirely identify, for I do already love, in that very identification. Thus does a mother truly love her children, just to the extent that she thinks of them as hers—not hers as possessions, the way material things might be hers, but hers as being a part of her very self. It only begins to be her duty to love them— which is really only pretending to love them—when this identification is eroded.

Acting as though the differences between myself and others did not matter is absolutely to acknowledge those differences. It is not love, but pretense, a really ugly imitation of love. It is not ugly of itself, since it is only an acknowledgement of difference, separateness, of an interpersonal chasm, and a resolution to act as though it were not there. There is nothing wrong with that, as such. It may even be essential to that type of social life we call (merely) civilized. But it is ugly if it is paraded as something *else,* namely love, for it is in fact a confession of lovelessness, and making the best of it.

The ugliness of such pseudolove is precisely the ugliness of everything specious. Thus, if something were paraded before us as an oracle, as a fountain of wisdom, and closer inspection revealed it to be nothing more than a jackass artfully decked out and dressed up to suggest learning and wisdom, the ugliness of the intended deception would be overwhelming. Again, if one were to approach the holy, only to have it turn out to be not merely profane, but a desecration of the holy, the ugliness would be sickening, and the more so if one were exhorted to pretend not to notice what was going on, to go through every motion of being in the presence of holiness and even roundly to declare it such.

In the same way, if one represents lovelessness, difference, the alienation of one soul from another, as an ultimate fact of existence, and then begs us to pretend not to notice it, to go through every motion of pretending to love, and even to declare that we do, the ugliness of the pretense is sickening. Seeking love, one is carried in the very opposite direction, and a wall is erected between oneself and the rest of creation

LOVE AND SEPARATION

—a wall that is made the more impenetrable by being rendered all but invisible.

The man who thinks that loving consists of treating others in a certain way, treating others according to certain formulae he has picked up—perhaps from his church, perhaps from his philosophy, it does not matter where—performs a double deception. He deceives not only a good part of the world, but himself as well. *He* thinks he loves the world. In fact he only treats the world in certain ways—as he might treat a pet dog or a child to which he thought he had certain obligations, as master or as father. Others are led also to think of all this as love, when it is nothing but rectitude, and thus do they come to think of love as something cold and even somewhat disagreeable. Because he has already mislabeled his rectitude, his decency, his sense of obligation, by giving these the name "love" and shining this light upon them for all to see, he not only makes it hard for others to love (for they think they have now seen what a cold thing it is), but he makes it impossible for himself.

If my hands are already filled with sand, and I think it is all gold, it is not possible for me to add gold to them, even if it is right at my feet; for I will not let go of what I have, nor can anything be added to it.

EMPIRICISM

We see everything through prisms. Nature has taught us to, for self-preservation; but the prisms are our own thought patterns. These prisms do not merely distort, they completely invert, so the fundamental truths, and what would otherwise be the most evident truths, sometimes appear false, and the most life-sapping falsehoods come to us as cold, stark, unassailable facts. Thus do the holy and the profane, love and alienation, the self and the world, and the whole of good and evil, get fairly turned around, each replacing its opposite, so that, hounded by our thought patterns, we endure monotony and loneliness. We imagine we are at least being faithful to fact, even to the truth, while the truth that nourishes is as bright and as restoring, when we have seen past crippling prisms, as the sands stretching off to the sky, the waves washing our feet and the sweet air in our throats.

The prismatic world is called fact, and the love of it, empiricism. Nature contemplated by a naked mind is called truth, and the love of it, mysticism. This love is also called metaphysics or sometimes, simply, religion; but it requires more than a superficial education to appreciate the propriety of this.

To the prismatic intellect, God is a distant being, so remote as to be beyond space and time altogether. God's love is not felt, and creation itself, which is as ubiquitous and eternal as the world, and as inescapable as the sunlight, is put back into a remote past where it becomes totally unbelievable, like everything else in religion conditioned by the refracting intellect. To such a mind belief is a pretense, and the lying profession of it an act of heroism. Thus does the prismatic, fractured, religious man confront you: stiff, frightened, upright, scrubbed, loveless, stupid. Speaking of holy love, he looks at you as though you were made of paper, a lifeless object, something to be scolded, warned, reproved and made to feel guilty for the very things you rejoice over. *His* god will scare the hell out of you, and *his* religious love will turn you to ice. He got that way because every fact in his universe contradicts him, actually denies that there is any god at all, denies that there is any love, even denies life itself—and he resents it. Why shouldn't he? But rather than blame the world, should he not blame his perception of it?

That is the first inversion: to represent God, whose reality is the only indubitable thing the mind can apprehend, as something problematical, indeed exceedingly doubtful, almost impossible, something requiring not merely heroism, but virtual madness, even to pretend to believe. And is it not dreadful? It evokes this utterly inadequate image: The child, sleeping profoundly in his mother's soft arms, gazed upon with deep, protective love and pride by his father—all the while dreaming, quivering in terror, madly thinking he is totally alone in a threatening world and on the very verge of obliteration! One does want to awaken the child with a soft kiss.

The mystic declares God to be perfectly obvious. The empiricist, with perfect understanding, breaks a clod of earth and says, "Is *that* a piece of God?" With still perfect understanding, he breaks an opening bud and asks, "Is *that* all you mean by creation?" With still perfect understanding, he points to the remote stars and to the grass and the woods and the oceans, and asks, "Is that what you mean by your *self?*" And the mystic has to reply, however in vain, "Yes— but it is you who have failed to see the clod, the bud, the heavens and the earth. You saw clearly enough, that if A is B, then B must be A— but while you began with the clod and then were lost in bafflement, I began with God and was lost in wonder. Talking about it isn't going to do either of us much good, though."

So there is the first inversion: turning the holy to the profane, then dashing about like a fool, seeing whether one can't find some reason to say something is holy. Of course the empiricist wants to know how you are going to prove that *you* haven't got it all backwards, to show *him* something new—on his terms, of course—when it all has nothing to do with showing anyone anything. It would be like asking the child to prove that that was only a dream he was having —perhaps his mother's arms were the dream! But they weren't, you know. It was the terror, not the love, that was dreamed.

The second inversion is that of love itself. Instead of seeing an identity, the empiricist sees the most manifest difference, distance, alienation—and the love of man, like the love of God, is transformed into something heroic, difficult, sacrificial, something for which one almost expects to be praised! For honesty and candor, put pretense. For the beauty of being warm, of smelling good, of being sometimes afraid; for the heartiness of laughter and the wrenching misery of tears; for being human, childish, genuine, real, substitute being a thing of papier-mâché, stiff, odorless, decorated, cold, dead, an interesting specimen, a toy.

It is as though the eye were to gaze condescendingly at the foot—a wretched thing condemned to walk in the dust and manure while the eye pursues a nobler destiny; or as though the right hand, so adroit, should feel pity and contempt for the left, so clumsy. Aristotle remarked that, apart from the man himself, the eye is no eye, any more than is the eye of a statue—though everyone calls this an eye. We sometimes speak as though, to be a man, it is only necessary to be born of man, to have the form characteristic of a man, to be a specimen, like the stiff, dry butterfly on a pin, the frog in the pickle jar. This is of course the empirical fact—that I am I, and you are you; that the world is one thing, and I am another; that the world is a collection of things of amazing variety, all distinct, quite totally distinct, separate, thrown together in a hodgepodge and collectively constituting a "world." That is a rather hard world to love. So it must take great effort to manage it. The man who loves the world must possess almost superhuman strength and courage. Yes indeed, if that is his view of it. The love that the unity of the world and God conveys as a gift, is withheld from the empiricist, no matter what his strength and courage. He can only imitate what others have found. But the strength, courage and heroism of the mystic are the strength, courage and heroism of a fly—and more than enough. Love is no matter of strength, it is only a matter of seeing, but seeing with an unblinded mind, a mind whose vision now includes not just color and form, but the odors of grasses and of wiggling things, and warm breath, and pine needles, and the nourishing ground; the sounds of water, wind, of rain and dry leaves, the feeling of gentle fingers, blanketing warmth, strong arms—all that shatters distance and separation, and that fills to overflowing instead of challenging, frightening and obliterating for the sake of self-preservation.

A Sunday school teacher once led all his children out of the stuffy church, where they were distracted and uneasy, and off to the woods. There he blindfolded every one and had them just sit on the ground and feel, without being able to look at, the pebbles, the plants, the earth. Not a word was said, not one single word, and when the blindfolds eventually came off, the children were startled to discover that every single hand was in the tight clasp of another's.

LONELINESS

A man's surface is his shell, and no snail has ever been so effectively protected, has more thoroughly excluded the world by withdrawing into its own exterior. The snail counts upon the physical cohesion of its shell, which is of course not unlimited. It takes rather little to break it down. But the human shell is invested with hardness by its owner and is psychological. Oddly, then, the shell that is impenetrable is the one composed by the spirit. The palpable shell of the snail is a bubble by comparison.

We are all just men standing elbow to elbow at the urinals in a Howard Johnson's restaurant. The distance between us is the distance between stars! Each is to his neighbor an object, a thing, an irritant whose existence is suffered because it cannot be helped. One draws in his spirit, shuts out the world—not because anything there really threatens, but just because it is there.

It is always easier to be alone or, failing that, at least to be able to feel alone, unfelt, unscrutinized, unappraised—and forsaken.

EGOISM

The egoist is simply a self-conscious man. Therefore, all are egoists, for no one for a moment forgets who he is, or has the least difficulty picking himself out, even in a crowded room. When one is speaking he is aware that he is speaking, though not perhaps aware how rudely or how foolishly. When one hears his own name, he is under no misconception whose name it is, as he sometimes is when it comes to the names of other people.

All of us are profoundly self-conscious, every one of us being acutely aware of himself at every moment, acutely concerned for himself, how he is faring in relation to the others around him, how he looks to them from moment to moment. It is in fact so natural for one to think of himself as an absolute center of the whole universe, and of everything else as simply the furniture of the world that is all *around* him, that for some it seems impossible ever to think otherwise or even to consider that any other metaphysics is even remotely possible.

The egoist's consciousness of himself is so absorbing that he is seldom able to become aware of other things, except in a derivative way, or in the manner in which they bear upon him, as presenting threat, promise or opportunity. Thus it is wholly impossible for the egoist to see an ant, for example, crawling across his desk without feeling a strong impulse to brush it off, an impulse that excludes any other response, even the response of curiosity, not to mention sympathy or even love. If he finds a nest of fledglings, his impulse is to run for a camera, that he might exploit this otherwise trivial situation for something of some use to himself. It is quite impossible, as impossible as the moon's ever reversing the direction of its orbit, that he should stare in wonder, even become intoxicated with deep, almost pitying love for these small beings, without, just for a moment, one single thought of himself; or (in a truly metaphysical transcendence) that he should discover his own soul in the small bits of wonderment that lie so clearly beyond the surface of his own skin.

Egoism seems characteristic of the transition from child to man, and is therefore childish only in that sense, that it characterizes the emergence from childhood. The child himself is only minimally self-conscious. He is capable of wonder, capable of staring at the most trivial things—at an insect, a fish, a remote star; even, sometimes it seems, at the air itself, or at clouds, or the sky. Men do not do these things; or at least it requires a great deal of piety for a man to think of doing them. The child has not arrived at the stage of fear and grasping, at the stage of manhood, where everything is contemplated through the prisms of question marks.

Are these things useful? Is there money in them? What can I do with them? It is not for the child a matter of doing. It is a matter simply of unself-conscious absorption. It would be dangerous for a man to go about things so dreamily. His day would seem almost endless. Very little would get done. It is partly this guilelessness, this innocence, aptly described as wide-eyed wonder, that gives childhood its charm. In their inward yearning for such wonder, such unself-consciousness, men are almost prepared to worship childishness. No sin seems quite so base as the corruption of a child's innocence, of his very childishness; and while most men seem to assume that this reverence for childishness is merely the desire to protect that which will someday grow to manliness, it is more likely that the gifts of innocence and wonder, of which the years rob us, are secretly envied—and rightly so.

Such innocence badly equips one for survival. Survival requires the shell that more than anything else distinguishes child from man. The world provides its substance, and its accretion is automatic. Things now come to be seen as *out there,* different, other; and as this perspective becomes clearer, so does another idea crystallize and become so firmly entrenched that no man can ever henceforth entirely shake it off, except in rare moments. This is the idea of the self, the ego. For one can hardly view the world as *out there,* except in relation to what is *not* out there, and that can be nothing but the ego. The idea of the *other* presupposes what is *not* other; and the *different,* what is the *same.* The whole thing is of course a myth, nothing more than a viewpoint acquired in the interest of survival, and yet it is so firmly embedded in our thought that even metaphysicians usually regard it as a datum, as something clearly given, rather than a problem, a puzzle, a fiction.

Thus is achieved the transition from childishness to manhood. It is a transition from belief to pretense, from sunlight to shadows, from naive candor to the most fantastically woven garments of make-believe, from faith to animalism— and yet it is thought absolutely necessary to make that transition, to blast the spirit out of everything, leaving brute matter, and to interpose walls throughout creation, precipitating small egos where before there were a god and a soul.

From now on the stars, the sky, snow-covered meadows and quiet groves, are no longer home, no longer warm and friendly. Home is four walls, and outside is the world. Living things—the insects one so patiently watched for hours without the least sense of patience, the minnows and snails that charmed one, that he seemed even to live and die with, the things of the grass and the air and the lake and forest— these are no longer things whose life is shared, but foreign things, other, beyond the self, beyond soul and spirit, things to be dealt with, used, looked at, sometimes hunted, even eaten. For the first object of life is not worship, but survival, and beyond that, the enhancement of what one has now discovered to be the ultimate reality, the basic reality, that to which all else is reduced, in terms of which all else has its meaning—and that is of course the self, the ego.

Now what before were realities, or childishly seemed so, move about one almost like shadows, things of form, but without substance, mere shapes, moving images that merely impinge upon one in various ways. A child is never astonished to see tears on the face of his father; it is quite natural, almost expected. But at the point when childishness has been put behind and self-consciousness has entered, the sight is shattering, almost like seeing a statue shedding real tears. It pierces for a moment that veil which has reduced the whole of otherness to a shadow existence; it momentarily reminds one of a common spirit, a common reality that makes no distinction between oneself and others. And for just this reason it is frightening, for it suggests that one of life's certainties, one of the premises of all philosophy and an article of most theology—namely, the ultimate reality of the self or private soul, and its absolute separation from whatever is not oneself—may be less than quite certain.

Reminders of this are of course everywhere: in the heavens at night, in the hills, in the woods and lakes; even in the tiniest things, in a single hair, a leaf or blade of grass. But it sometimes takes something shattering to force one to heed them, something like seeing one's father crying, as though a statue could feel. Then it is not egoism that blasts the spirit out of everything, but sympathy that, in spite of one's efforts, fears and mortification, blasts a hole, a brief hole, in the wall of separateness that has been erected by our own defensive egoism.

THE ETERNAL

We are the creation of God, though nothing but form arose with our birth nor will perish with our death. Our being is not something grasped hazardously, not something rationed, augmented or diminished, according to what we deserve; nor does it belong to an immortal soul we carry within us, as one might, for security, carry a gold-piece in his pocket.

Being is epitomized, not by impenetrable rocks, but by waves spreading themselves over the surface of the sea. These perfectly exemplify change, and the eternally changeless. Our stone edifices and monuments express our wishes, not our perceptions. We raise them skyward as though to remove them from the world of decay, as if to point to the permanence of heaven, as though to establish, here and there, specks of immutability that not even an eternity can corrupt, so deeply do we crave something that will remain. Our monuments are as large as we can make them, though we know they are still only specks, and we make them of granite, though we know that time will reduce them to the elements as inevitably as a raindrop is dispersed.

What captivates the metaphysician in this is not the illusory character of what is sought, for the eternal and changeless is certainly not an illusion; but rather, the inappropriateness of its symbols. A rock, a monolith, a temple, a granite arch, these are transient things. We know this. By what, then, shall we represent the eternal, if not by these imperfect means?

Oddly enough, this very eternity and changelessness, even the unchanging God, are beautifully symbolized by the turbulent sea, ever changing and yet ever the same. Here is our model of being and of creation. In the picture one finds himself, too, as a part of that creation. Here one sees mortality expressed, not in a unique origination *ex nihilo* and a unique extinction, but rather in our perpetual regeneration, shared by the entire creation. A wave, a raindrop, a waterfall, a person, a rock, a star, is at no two instants the same wave, drop or whatever. All existence, excepting God only, is instantaneous. Yet this arising and passing exists only on the surface, like the ocean waves. Beneath it nothing has arisen and nothing has gone.

Plato looked at the world and saw nothing but change, and therefore, he thought, decay, a continuous lapsing from reality. The world of sunrises and sunsets, of seasons, of birth and death, is at no two moments the same. Like the ocean, what it is is constantly changing into what it is not, and every earthly thing partakes of this mutability. Plato saw rocks and mountains, the heavens themselves, drifting constantly from being to nothingness. This world of matter cannot then, he thought, be real. It at best resembles or

THE ETERNAL

partakes of reality. The real, he was quite correctly convinced, is the changeless, the same from age to age. Its symbol is no mutable thing, such as a rock, of whatever durability, but rather, the changeless idea, the form, something divorced from everything mundane. Nor, he declared, is our mortality an ultimate fact, for this belongs to our bodies, which lie in the world of sense, and not to our inner souls. If we must have a symbol of reality from the world of sense, Plato suggested, we should look to the sun—something far removed from the earth, and the source of pure and inexhaustible light, in which no darkness, symbolic of nonbeing, is mingled. Even so, it is an imperfect symbol, for like everything grasped by sense, it is subject to change.

Plato should, however, have sought the eternal, not in his own supposed ego, mind or soul, nor in metaphysical abstractions that are sundered from nature, but in nature herself—not, indeed, in nature created, but in nature creating.

That the eternal might be epitomized by the sea, by that very perfection of ceaseless change, could never have been the least credible to Plato. And it is, indeed, at first hard to grasp, really about the last thing that would occur to one. It is no wonder men have invented the myth of heaven and the myth of the soul. Yet once this simile is understood, it can never be surrendered.

A wave moves over the face of the ocean. We can see it, distinguish it from another, even touch it and trace its brief history. It arises at a particular place, a particular time, swells, moves steadfastly, breaks—and is gone forever. But in truth no wave has moved at all. In truth the undulations of the water are vertical, not horizontal. It only seems that something has moved over the surface. A given wave is at one moment so entirely distinct from what it, the "same" wave, was a moment before, that it may share not one common element with its predecessor. All that has arisen, moved over the surface and then perished, is a shape, a modification. We call it a thing, and could even, if there were a point to it, give it a name. If conscious, it could assert "I think; I am." But that which affirmed "I think" would not be what affirmed "I am," except in form only. What there is, is the sea, here and there momentarily modified by waves, and while it is at no two moments the same, it still remains forever the same, changeless, eternal, its transient variations continuing from age to age.

ALIENATION

The illusions of separateness, autonomy and pluralism give rise to the deepest yearning of men and at the same time to incredibly inappropriate efforts to fulfill it. The yearning is to be loved. The means by which men endeavor to attain this love are loaded with the comedy that characterizes all ineptitude, all misguided effort or ill choice of means, and at the same time with the sadness of a seemingly invincible stupidity. One wants to laugh and to cry, as one does watching a clown who fills one's eyes with tears; and one is not quite sure in the end that they were tears of laughter.

Love is the perception of identity, and one who sees God and the world in this way has no greater need to be loved by other things, than to love them, for these things have ceased to be other and have also ceased to be things. Both needs are overwhelming, but both are fulfilled. The perception does not cancel the need to be loved, except by total satiation. Hence instead of rendering the philosopher cold and aloof, self-sufficient and uncaring, the perception fills him with warmth and makes him once more a part of the world instead of a parasite upon it. The craving for self-sufficiency is abolished when the limited and autonomous self disappears from view, and caring ceases to be a passion of desperation. Love is something on which to recline; to the extent that one frantically pursues it, he has already lost it. The man who spans the globe looking for the one true light, losing his way because he is blinded by the light that keeps shining in his eyes, is not likely to find anything that was worth seeking.

If I think of myself as a separate being, I at once become, to myself, a center of existence. "Here" becomes simply where I am, and, without thinking about it, I seem to myself to be the only person, virtually the heart of creation. All else, the universe in its vastness, even God, is "out there," and is an "it," a vast thing, rather than a "thou." The separateness with which I perceive myself produces a gulf between me and all else, between the ego and a vast, cold, uncaring otherness. And of course the gulf is not one I can ever step across, for it is metaphysical, the creation of my own thought.

How, then, will a man's yearning to be loved find expression under such a conception? In two obvious ways, both perfectly familiar and both clearly destined to fail. The first is what may be broadly called self-ornamentation; and the second, the effort to possess. Both are ridiculous, and yet one can hardly help pitying those whose madness devises them.

If I am a separate being and hence entirely other than you, then my only hope for satisfying my yearning will be through some sort of appearance of greatness. I must appear as a kind of wonder, a jewel, a thing of beauty. I must in a word rise above the rest of creation as best I can or, since that is obviously impossible, I must appear to. Thus will I awe all others and, through being awe-inspiring, be loved. But here suddenly the absurdity leaps up. By seeking to be loved, I have established the very conditions that make it impossible, for no one has ever loved that by which he is awed and from which he thus felt far removed. This is in fact the exact description of the defeat of love. Love is not engendered by unique beauty, but by the very plainness that unites everything; it is not nourished by what sets its object apart, but by what reaches across that apartness. The face of love that is felt, that is warm, that abolishes time, space and multiplicity, is a homely face.

Hence failing to impress, one tries to possess. But possession is by nature the acknowledgment of difference and alienation; what I possess, I cannot love, except in a figurative sense. I can only grasp or selfishly hold it. It is not impossible, for example, for a father to love his son; but if he thinks of his son as one of his possessions, or even as his greatest possession, then love for him is impossible. To possess is to use, to subordinate to one's own will, to add on to oneself, to exploit; and nothing like this can even form the smallest part of loving. It entirely rules it out. Therefore, possession of one person by another, even if it should be complete, makes love of that person impossible, by its very success. It is not love, nor a form of love, but a replacement of love, resembling loving only by the presence of concern for the thing possessed. But the concern is misleading; it is really only a concern for oneself, as distinct. "I love you" cannot, under these conditions, ever become "I love thee," for "thee" must denote more than a thing, and what is possessed cannot be more than a thing to its possessor.

SELF-LOVE

An overwhelming love for oneself can be either the most cramping, shrinking and sickening passion one can suffer, or it can, on the contrary, lead to an immeasurable love for the whole of being, which is simply God and creation together. It is odd that one and the same passional state could lead to such utterly antipodal effects, but it is not hard to see how this happens if one considers the possibilities.

The manner in which self-love leads to self-isolation and loneliness is fairly obvious. Consider the tyrant—master of the fates of millions, known and feared by most of the world—who craves the affection of his small daughter and only barely finds any of it. This is certainly a curious image. But we need no such extreme example, particularly if it suggests that there is anything rare and unusual in what it is intended to convey. Simply look about you, at the man who devotes almost his whole energy to increasing his possessions, these growing to a veritable mountain while his inner self shrivels to a nut, totally unloved, totally abandoned by the world he strives so hard to impress. Or think of the scholar, peerless, awesome to the learned world, envied on every side, but nowhere loved, and even resented by his own sons who would rather die than follow in his steps. He has, from self-love, tried to enhance his own being by adding to its ornamentation. He does not differ, inwardly, from the tyrant or the man of boundless possessions.

The image here is familiar, easy to grasp. Its basic element is this: A man is driven by an overwhelming self-love—a state containing, as noted, the potentialities for either heaven or hell. He therefore craves insatiably the love of others, which is absolutely not to be condemned, since this is a craving for what is quite rightly seen to be divinely good. But then he goes about things in the most obvious way, which also turns out to be the most misguided: He seeks to embellish himself by greatly enlarging that part of the world that he can influence, impress, even overpower. By doing this he makes an absolute distinction between himself and that world, so that, as the portion of the latter which he can call *his* increases, the very self he thinks of as at its center becomes reduced to nothing. If anyone were to look for the man anymore, he would immediately find himself in a vast and impenetrable sea of what is not the man, of that with which the man has surrounded himself in the vain hope that he can enlarge his own being by enlarging what he can attach himself to. The result is the exact opposite of what he intended. He is like a spider spinning its web from its own substance, so that as the web gets larger and impenetrable, its source at the center must inevitably shrivel up. The spider becomes no grander as its web increases;

it is precisely that which is not the spider that spreads itself out.

Men are not unaware of this danger, and some have responded by condemning self-love itself. One must not, they think, love himself, but should *instead* love everyone and everything else. Some even represent this as a duty. Some even suppose that in fulfilling it one must put on a sad and sober face, as though the love for others is painful, requiring one's own self-rejection. Some even virtually invite the world to urinate on them, thinking that love should be self-sacrificial and needing some dramatic proof of the extent to which self-sacrifice and self-rejection can go.

All this springs from an illusion. Those who, from self-love, seek fulfillment of their craving for love by ornamenting themselves, adding to their possessions, power or status, labor under an illusion. Those who, correctly perceiving that this approach miscarries, seek fulfillment of their craving for love in the opposite way, by self-abasement and self-abnegation, labor under exactly the same illusion.

The illusion is simply that of a self, an ego, at the center of a world, the whole of which is thus seen as something *other*.

There is indeed the self, the ego. If there were not, it could hardly be loved. But paradoxically, that self, that ego, is not distinct from that realm we think of as other. The distinction between the *I* and the *you,* between the *me* and the *it*—between, in short, oneself and the world—is only one of degree. It is not an absolute distinction between two beings. Hence mystics who have thought of themselves as absorbed by the divine were not fools. They have only expressed in a joyous, perhaps melodramatic way, their own liberation from this great illusion.

DIVINE LOVE

There is a love that crumbles conceit like a sand pillar. Enmity becomes an insubstantial shadow; pride bows impotently. The beholder of this love is not converted to a servant of man, nor filled with the zeal for good works. He is stunned to helplessness.

We have seen this love, in a convict, ragged, his body broken, dirty, sweating, humiliated, defeated. It is no wonder we beheld this glory and said: God became man.

In that setting we glimpsed an unmotivated love that inverts all human good and evil.

Do not say: "How inspiring!"

Do not say: "How noble!"

Do not say: "How unselfish!"

These are just ways of saying: How human! That is to miss the point.

But what is it?

No doubt Jesus loved mankind, just as we at least sometimes do. When tested, he seemed to pass the tests: defending the whore, and that sort of thing. But do not point to him in praise of that love. History provides plenty of examples of it that are just as good. You see it often yourself. You even feel it yourself, and with justified pride. But it is not what we are talking about.

We would like to think that the love of mankind—the love that moves the upright and honorable, the love that puts strangers ahead of oneself, that trusts, that kindles light—we would like to think that this is godlike, and find it confirmed in the Gospels. It is so utterly human. It fuels conceit.

But Jesus did not say: "Through this hideous suffering something will be made better."

He did not say: "Through this, others will be improved."

He did not say: "By this, even my enemies will be ennobled."

Or even: "They will see the light."

He did not say: "I shall love them and thereby redeem them."

He did not even say: *"I* forgive them." This would have been a vain and human performance.

That is not the love that stuns.

There is a human love more garish than jewels and gold capes. It poses and postures. It is as if its possessor were before a mirror, never tiring of the sight. He radiates love for the world and mankind. This love smiles unspontaneously, the fixed smile of a statue, and its smiles are blandishments.

Such love fairly screams: "Behold, a loving person."

It says: "I find goodness and light everywhere."

DIVINE LOVE

It says: "Count on me—decent, righteous, loving."

Its energy is as boundless as its vanity. The wearer of this love has forsaken every customary ornament. He displays whatever is plain—plain garb, plain grooming, plain face, and through all, a plain smile that never fades, is never canceled by self-doubt, nor by tears.

And through this studied plainness, meticulous simplicity, carefully, elaborately contrived, there glows the self-approbation that fairly blinds the beholder.

This love would evaporate like the summer fog if it were not in the tight grasp of the lover.

He says: "Here am I, loving mankind."

He says: "Here am I, repudiating things weak."

He says: "Here am I, helping even the unworthy."

He says: "Here am I, acting like Jesus!"

All that is lacking is the mirror.

Such love is insufferable to all but its exhibitor, whom it intoxicates.

But had Jesus smiled, the thing would soon have been forgotten.

Had no tears or anguish been there, the thing would have been forgotten.

Had he pretended that even these were good men, somehow worthy of the love that implies approbation, the episode would soon have been forgotten. And gladly.

What, then, is it?

Jesus did not say: "Forgive them, they do not really mean it."

He said: "Forgive them, they are ignorant."
Nor did he feign humility or servitude.
He did not claim to be innocent, or good, or wise.
He thought of himself as a god—which is hardly the mark of abject humility.

Divine love is an apprehension. The beloved self vanishes from the scene altogether. It is not the love of one man for another, for the otherness has ceased to exist. It is not abject, humble, sacrificial, but godlike. It does not do things, it need not even say anything. It merely sees. And this is what is so incredible, just the last thing one would have expected: that love, a love that does not enliven but stuns, should be nothing more than a certain apprehension.

But this is not seeing as an observer. One sees, with heart and mind.

MONISM

If one affirms an identity or unity of life and existence, it must be there, or otherwise one will be only fabricating a pleasant fairy tale. To say that life is one, that all of creation is a unity, that the world is one with God—such things may, as slogans, serve a certain purpose, but, one is likely to think, they have no place in philosophy. For obviously, distinctness, difference, separation and plurality are no less basic features of the world than day and night. To deny them is simply to deny fact.

Here one fails to see that these facts are simply human creations. We find it useful, even necessary for certain purposes, to view the world in certain ways, to affix labels and markers to enable us better to deal with it. Then we forget where these labels and markers came from and imagine they are part of reality, now discovered by us.

Thus, we affirm that a certain area of land, indistinguishable from the rest, is the property of this or that man. And such an affirmation may indeed be correct, may state a fact; the man named may in fact hold title to that land. But it is obviously a fact created by men in the pursuit of certain ends.

The world was not created with this area already demarcated and bearing signs identifying its owner. If one man were to declare the area in question indistinguishable from those adjoining, while another declared it to be clearly distinct in terms of its ownership, neither would really be wrong; they would only be describing things at different levels.

Much of the seeming conflict between metaphysics and common sense is, similarly, a difference of the levels at which things are viewed. It is the first aim of metaphysics to see things in ways that are not just human creations, to overcome the tendency to view the derivative as though it were original.

Consider for example the tree that stands outside my window. It is an ancient apple, and as I contemplate it, I can distinguish ever so many of its numberless leaves; similarly, the stems, twigs and branches leading to these, then back down to the trunk and into the earth. Now if I pick out one of those leaves, it seems perfectly natural and correct to say: That is one leaf, distinguishable from all the rest, and distinguishable, too, from the twigs, branches and the tree on which it grows. If this particular leaf were to fall, the rest would remain, unaffected. The tree is very old, but the leaf is not; it came into being but a few weeks ago, and in a few more it will perish, though the tree will remain. The tree, therefore, is one thing, and this leaf, another; and the same can be said of the rest of the leaves, similarly of the many stems, twigs, branches, and all the tree's other many separate and distinct parts.

That seems natural enough, even obvious; but it is not the

truth of things. The distinctness, separation and plurality that I see here are the creation of my own eyes and my own habits of thought. My thinking is not metaphysical, but practical. I have drawn certain distinctions, I have in my mind cut the tree up into parts, because this is a useful way to view it. And then I have supposed that these distinctions are my discoveries, that in affirming them I am merely affirming reality as it in fact is. As I label the various things "leaf," "twig" and so on, I forget where the labels originally came from, and I speak as though they were put there by nature herself.

This can be seen very clearly as soon as we note that the manner in which I have drawn these distinctions is only one of infinitely many, any of which would have had as much and as little foundation as the one suggested. Thus, having distinguished leaves, I could have distinguished halves of these, or any other fractional parts, and treated such parts as separate beings. The temptation is of course to protest that a half a leaf is only an artificially discriminated part of a whole leaf, not something that exists in its own right. Somehow one does not at first feel the same impulse to say that a leaf itself is only an artificially discriminated part of a tree, not something existing in its own right.

As our intellect divides, for whatever purposes, so also of course it can combine. Still using the same example, we could, for instance, consider any two leaves that touch, as one thing, giving it a name; and the same for any three or four. We could then regard the separation of such beings into constituent leaf parts as the dissolution of the things in question.

Such ways of viewing familiar things seem arbitrary and whimsical, but that is only because we happen to have no uses for such distinctions. When we make them, to illustrate a metaphysical point, we find we have no names at hand to bestow on the beings thus concocted. Where, however, did such familiar names as leaf, twig, branch and even tree itself come from? Were they not invented by men, in response to practical needs? And whence came the pronouns me, you, it, and the names God, the world, and the possessives, mine and thine? Did God go to all the trouble of creating these for us? When Descartes said with such certainty, "I exist," was his certainty vouchsafed by God? Where did he even get the pronoun necessary for making the assertion?

Suppose we now go another step. Let us imagine each leaf of our tree is conscious, aware of itself, and views itself as we view it, and follows the metaphysical train of thought to which that view inevitably gives rise. Its thought is, I exist; I am one among many of my kind, all distinct from me as I from them; I came into being, was affixed to a tree, from which I draw my nourishment, and at some time I shall perish and become nothing again, though others like me will take my place.

Such a reflection expresses, of course, how virtually all men think of themselves in relation to others and to the world. We can see the limitation and falsity of such a conception, when applied to the leaf. It is somehow less obvious when we apply it to ourselves. We see well enough that the leaf is not a parasitic growth on the tree, but part of it. The tree does not nourish it as a separate being; rather, the tree and its parts are nourished. The leaf was not affixed to the tree, much less did anything like this happen at some point in time. Nor will it ever perish or become nothing; that which it is, it has always been and will always be, though under numberless appearances. We name some of the appearances —now leaf, now bud, now decay, and so on—but even God could not literally reduce to nothing what we thus diversely refer to. We can say, if we like, that in any case the *apparent* leaf will become nothing, but that is not very surprising when we realize that it was never more.

It is fanciful to imagine an apple leaf acquiring consciousness and the power of reason—though hardly more strange than to consider a man doing this. We see, right off, what the leaf's first thought is going to be. We see, right off, what is going to follow from it. We see a metaphysic unfold with the inevitability of night, then turn to engulf its very creator in darkness. "I exist"—the first step; "in my own right"—the second step; "and thus to seize all I can in the endeavor to perpetuate my own being, even at the expense of everything else and even, indeed, at the expense of God, if need be"— and so on, to the terribly bitter end.

ARISING

What is our earth but dead remains, lifeless, inert, the accretions of millennia; and yet, how beautiful. She is both mother and tomb, ineluctably taking what she has herself given, at once the goddess who quickens and the reaper, hurrying everything on to the silence of oblivion, that others may have their turn. Some soon, some later—but each will have his turn, his moment, his escape from nothingness, to compensate for his eternal return to it.

Millions of seasons creep by, earth relentlessly rolling, mountains swelling skyward through age after age and washing down like sand castles over more ages, continents rising and sinking, glaciers pressing forth, receding—until finally, at an exact place and an exact time, a miracle: the merest gnat takes form. It lives out the details of its history moment to moment, and perishes utterly. At long last it has had its turn, for a while it *was,* it filled a definite small space through a definite small time, and then forever, it was nothing again. A real being arose, exactly as though, from its point of view, all that preceded was preparation, preliminary, rehearsal and stage setting for that final emergence, from zero, of itself—

something absolutely real, in a space and in a time, and then absolutely nothing again, but this time, forever.

But this is no vision of reality. It is the empiricism of a gnat, of contemptible significance; or of a man, perhaps, who boasts that reality will have to be just what it looks like—which means whatever catches the eye of this or that of its ephemeral expressions.

But being is not encompassed in the reality of a gnat, nor in that of a man. Assuredly not in your own.

One might drop a pebble into a pond, perhaps in the still and dark of the night, and declare, with truth, that the splash was ever so real, unmistakable, one would be deaf not to hear it; or that the glint and sparkle of the stars in the ripples were so manifest, so perfectly real, one would be blind not to see them; or that the ripples themselves could be counted, one could distinguish this one from that, note how many there were, say just when one began, when it ended, and where—but have you ever tried that?

And there *are* the pond, the enveloping darkness, the silence, the earth, the stars, God and the angels of heaven. Need one be a metaphysician to find them?

PERISHING

Men fear nothingness and dread its approach. But unlike other threats, this one can never be stayed, nor fled, not in the least, not even if one were given all the powers of heaven. Nothing gives it an instant's pause; nothing can. Its approach is as certain as the changing of the seasons; indeed, far more so. And to add to its terror, it is immense; for in truth it is infinite in every way possible. There is nothing relative about it. It opens, like a vast abyss, as with the fading of each pulse it draws nearer. It presents itself to the mind as the most total certainty, next to which even the existence of the heavens and the earth seems tenuous, fragile. When millions of years have elapsed, when new mountains have arisen, new canyons been eroded from rock, new stars born and finally become extinguished, the nothingness that shall have consumed us will not have been diminished in the least. If one imagines a grain of sand on an endless, empty plain, he will still have no adequate comparison of his existence to the immensity of his nonexistence. One feels that it would be satisfying to exchange the two, to possess an existence as boundless as that nothingness, to reduce that all-enveloping nothingness to the dimensions of one's own ephemeral being. Sometimes men wish this so profoundly that they even assert that it is so, on the testimony of nothing but theologians.

Yet the strange thing about this thought, this ultimate certainty and inexorable necessity, is that it is purely the creation of the human imagination, without any truth whatsoever. That very existence, that soul or ego, which theologians tempt us to hope might be more durable than appearances suggest, is itself already a part of the nothingness which the theologians so ingeniously seek to avoid. And this puts us in a strange and paradoxical position, that the existence with which we are so deeply concerned, the existence that seems threatened with obliteration, the existence to which we try to cling, by every means, including even the profession of absurdities, is not even real to begin with! We struggle, by hope, by faith, by metaphysics, to keep alive a flame that has never cast the smallest ray. Obsessed with a chimera, we fail to see that what is inexorable and infinite, that which we are, from which we come and to which we assuredly go, is not nothingness, but its very opposite, which is being, or God. It would be impossible to imagine things turned more thoroughly upside down, and it is no wonder men dwell so much in emotional doldrums, that they are so terrified and sick in their hearts and try vainly to add to their existence simply by adding to their power over the rest of creation. Nothing like this is in the least called for. That, whose extinction each dreads, has no reality to start with. We need, therefore, not fear its loss.

For from what do you recoil? From annihilation, the reduction to nothingness. The annihilation of what? Consider a leaf, a blade of grass, an insect. Does it depress you that these might perish, or inevitably will, and very soon? Does the durability of a pebble, by comparison, fill you with comfort? No; these are insignificant things. It does not matter whether they are or are not, or whether they have ever been. They are of no account, they exist by the millions and perish by the millions at every moment; they mean nothing.

Then what of things that are not insignificant—persons, for instance, or even nations? That one of these should perish is no small thing. But is their nothingness what you dread? Consider the countless millions upon millions who have gone before you. Does it matter? Are you appalled by the mortality of a single one? Consider even nations that have arisen and vanished. You know now only their names, and only a tiny few of these; the rest do not matter much any more. Surely their extinction, though perhaps sad if one takes a moment to think of it, presents no hint of the terror and dread felt a moment ago.

In short it is this: That things should arise and perish perpetually, that this mutation should be as apparent as existence itself, and inseparable from it—this appalls no one, this presents no overwhelming fact driving some men to depression and madness, others to religion, and virtually all to greed and grasping for power. At most, it puzzles, perhaps depresses, a metaphysician, who would prefer the reality of spirit, immutability, even timelessness. And matter itself—

sometimes lovely, sometimes ugly, always in motion—never disturbs us, just as such. It is the approaching nothingness that does this, the sense of our mortality; we feel our very being slipping away, irrecoverable, a thought perfectly symbolized by the sandglass, with its steady replacement of being with nothingness. Here we seem to see reality slipping away, and then its final, total extinction.

The nothingness that sickens and appalls, the nothingness we would give anything to drive back, if only for a while, is only our own. The perishing of other things, even other persons, even persons loved, saddens and of course carries the acute reminder of what awaits us. But it is this last, alone, that fills us with dread. Dying and then being dead, being no more, being nothing—why this total calamity? Why this, to crown the most beautiful of lives? Lucky the beasts, who fear, but know not what they fear. We know; it is not concealed from us; we know with the same stark realization as the prisoner being ushered towards the gallows.

Lucretius tried to overcome this problem by proclaiming what he took to be the fact of his own approaching extinction, but extracting its terror through abstruse metaphysics. That which in no way exists, he said, can in no way suffer any evil, so one's own conversion to nothingness is no evil to be dreaded. As no one laments the ages that elapsed without him, so no rational being will resent the approach of more such ages to come. Nothingness is no state of evil; it is, rather, no state at all, hence nothing to dread, nothing to wish to flee or resist.

But there is something lugubrious to Lucretius' metaphysics, however incontestable may be his claims, at a metaphysical level. As that which in no way is, can suffer no evil, so also that which rejoices, must be. It is not the pain and anguish of nothingness that threatens; it is, simply, the conversion to nothingness. And Lucretius has not made this less dreadful. No special claims need be made of the blessings of existence. There may be none; but existence itself is usually felt as a good—sometimes outweighed by the evils attending it, to be sure, but nevertheless, as a good, quite apart from its being a precondition of all goodness. And nonexistence is a deprivation. Lucretius surely did not, in representing death as the transition to sheer nothingness, thereby remove its sting in the least. Concede to him that what in no way exists can suffer no pain. This renders inexhaustible nothingness hardly more inviting.

What, then, do we know? What is it that is thought to be so clearly displayed to us, but concealed from the beast? Indeed, I do know that *I am*. Do I know, too, that I shall *not be?* It entirely depends on *what* I am.

The terrible fact of an approaching nothingness, which we fancy ourselves to know, was born only of our own brains, the fruit of our dissecting intellects—intellects that pulverize the whole of being into bits, make independent existences of each of these, forthwith conceive ourselves as identical with this one or that, and then draw back in terror to "realize" that every single one, *including that one,* is subject to decay.

It is the self that each of us sees destined for oblivion. We do not mind that a billion others await the same fate, that more billions have gone to it; it is the fate of one's *own* self that concerns him. That and that alone—that is the crux. But what if this very self should already belong to that nothingness we somehow dread? Would that not put a rather different aspect on our philosophy? Instead of prattling what everyone surely knows to be false—that this dear self will vanquish nothingness, that it will be right there forever, that the extinction that awaits everything else will pass over it so that it will not perish—instead of saying such things, let us consider: What *are* we talking about?

One imagines that he is deeply, perpetually, unavoidably aware of something he calls "I" or "me." The philosopher then baptizes this thing *self* or perhaps his *mind,* and the theologian calls it his *soul.* It is, in any case, something that is at the very heart of things, the very center of reality, that about which the heavens and the firmament revolve. But should not one feel embarrassment, to talk in such a way or even to play with such thoughts? As soon as one begins to try saying anything whatever about this inner self, this central reality, he finds he can say nothing at all. It seems to elude all description. All one can do, apparently, is refer to it; one can never say what is referred to, except by multiplying synonyms—as if the piling of names upon names would somehow guarantee the reality of the thing named! But as soon as even the least description is attempted, one finds that what is described is indistinguishable from absolute nothingness. Then when one realizes that he began by fearing nothingness, that it was this invincible nothingness that was making him miserable, driving him towards madness—when one goes back, and reviews his thought and feeling, and finds it leading to the most familiar thing imaginable—one feels like a child caught making faces at himself in the mirror; one feels like a child plunged into anxiety by a skin blemish or ill-fitting pants: the absurdity is so overwhelming.

There seem to be two realities—myself and all the rest. By "all the rest" is meant the whole of creation, except me. (It should already be apparent that this is a very strange way to begin philosophy!) This rest, this everything else, all that is outside, other, is perpetually changing, never for two moments the same. But at the heart of it all, at that point which is the metaphysical center of reality, is that self, that which is not something "else"—and it does *not* change, or at least does not become something *else*. It remains one and the same, throughout all the changes it suffers, preserving its identity through an ever-lapsing and growing time. Except for this: that it does finally suffer that calamitous change, which is its own extinction! And that is a pretty awesome thought, a dreadful thought, a cosmic insult.

All right, now let us track down this being, whose reduction to nothingness we are trying to cope with and find some comfort for. We can begin with things that are manifestly *not* the self, things that are most clearly other, as distant from the self as possible. So we begin with the heavenly bodies, work down to the oceans and mountains and drifting clouds. These are *not* myself, not the thing I am seeking. Let us move in closer—to loved ones, things near at hand, the familiar, one's own house, table, bed, the things around one. We seem to be getting closer. Now the body itself—limbs, senses, organs, internal and external parts, nerves—all this, we could go on and on. We are *very close* now; but these are all, still, other—these are not the self I am seeking, whose destruction I dread, except insofar as the destruction of these threatens myself. *So now we take that final step,* from all that is other, from all that I merely know or see, or that merely pertains to me; we take that last step, from all this to my self, to that which perceives all the rest, to that in relation to which all these things are called other. And lo! We step precisely to nothingness! Is it not a bit of a shock to one learned in philosophy? That self, which we took for the ultimate reality, the central reality, that self whose being we took to be least susceptible to question, is not even there. No magic, no miracle, no science, no metaphysics, nothing whatever can conjure it up, nothing can produce the smallest semblance of what we were going to display. We were chasing a will-o'-the-wisp. We wanted something to present as an ultimate reality, to contrast with everything else, and we found total, perfect nothingness! That ultimate reality isn't there. Imagination creates it. Intellect distinguishes it. Metaphysics builds intellectual fortresses upon it. Religion guarantees its salvation—always of course on certain terms— and promises to push back the nothingness that approaches it. And all the while, it is itself the most perfect specimen of nothingness! One does indeed feel like a child discovered making a face at himself in the mirror. One wants somehow to cover up what was going on, he is so embarrassed at his own ridiculousness.

Then what *am* I? For I surely exist. Try this: Instead of starting with the heavens and firmament, mountains and oceans and drifting clouds, with things, and peeling all these away in vain search for something somehow *more precious* at their center, do the opposite. Instead of withdrawing inwards, towards some imagined bit, some atom (which will surely slip away the moment you think you have it)— instead of this, try to proceed outwards and see heaven and earth, mountains and oceans and drifting clouds, all you have been taught to regard as things, as others, as foreign and distant, see all these as they are. You will be momentarily astonished to find yourself, God and nature; and far from dreading nothingness, which now seems like sickness and hardly worthy of anyone, which is how you began all this, your state of mind will be just the opposite. You will rejoice in being, in God, in yourself, which will now have ceased to be any mystery, and you will finally understand what it means to love them.

THE ILLUSION OF SELFHOOD

Appreciating the force of an illusion seldom has any power to abolish the illusion itself. It persists, no matter how clearly and how indubitably the understanding discerns its illusory character. Thus the illusory self, like the face in the mirror, gazes back at one, mimicking his very denials of its reality. Understanding that there is really nothing there does not obliterate the lively appearance. One might even reason, absurdly, that there must be *something* there, for what, otherwise, is it that mocks one? Philosophers have actually said this sort of thing. The realization that an illusion can be *total* is sometimes not easily won.

The stars seem tiny to the child, sparkling grains of silver he can almost grasp by the handful and scatter like sand. They seem no less tiny when he comes to understand that they are in fact immense things. He has lost only the temptation to reach for them. The illusion persists unabated, though it is no longer acted upon. The rainbow, similarly, seems no less definite and no less exactly placed, merely because we have learned the physical principles of refraction. An uninstructed person might seek it out, might even want to touch it. When we say that there is no rainbow there, it is not always convincing, even to ourselves. We do, after all, see it. The understanding of truth does not diminish the illusion's presence and beauty, and we even want to say that in some sense there really is a rainbow there, that it is not a total illusion. But still, it is.

Thus I can declare, and my understanding can accept the truth of it, that this finite and mortal self, for which I have so intense a regard, this existential center of everything, is in fact nothing. I can say it, affirm it, believe it without any doubt whatever—but the illusion has not been diminished at all. It is like the face I see in the mirror. Even as I deny that it exists, it seems to mock my very denial. Yet what I say is true; there is no self there. It only seems to be there.

It was this power of an illusion to make intelligible discourse that so enchanted Descartes. "I doubt that I exist," he said, and having said it, he was captivated by his inability to mean it. The echo always came back, "I exist." Descartes was therefore unable to sustain his doubt. And because the doubt was thus seemingly overwhelmed, he mistook the victor in this contest to be the metaphysical certainty of his self. "I do not exist" *cannot* be true, he thought. So the denial of this negation must be true. Hence certain. But he did not stop to consider that the apparent image in a mirror could have said the same thing, and thereupon could have proceeded through the same strange performance.

Illusions are thus penetrated or seen through, but not banished. When we greet someone in the darkness, only to discover that we are addressing our own reflection in a glass, we stop speaking to it, but it does not leave. The same is true with respect to the evanescent rainbow and the flickering stars overhead, so that the claims of sense and understanding are thrown into a battle in which neither prevails. The same is true with respect to the finite self, which will always seem to its possessor to be the primal reality, more basic even than the world, less doubtful even than God. One can eventually come to see that it is a fiction, but one can never have the least hope of vanquishing it.

One can accordingly not really live as though that inner self, that central contemplator of the world, that ego, were nothing. This would be like expecting the rainbow to vanish at one's command. The nuclear self will always seem to be the thing that really matters. Thus what matters, it seems to me, are *my* thoughts, *my* feelings, *my* consciousness, and even, *my* dreams and illusions—but do not be mistaken about this. What is being talked about in such a declaration are not thoughts, feelings or dreams, but their supposed possessor. There were thoughts and feelings long before I appeared on the scene, and they will continue long after I leave. That does not matter to me. What counts is precisely the "me," the ego, my self. It counts less when seen to be an illusion, certainly, but no metaphysics will ever make it seem the least less real. For this reason the wisest man must act like the fool. Only his thoughts will be different, and these only at those rather rare times when he is able to be philosophical. Otherwise, just as the fool does, he will show off, prefacing everything with the thought, "Here am I." Thus: "Here am I, strong and powerful," and "Here am I, learned," and "Here am I, envied," and "Here am I, a veritable star." Even his gravestone someday will proclaim, "Here am I, take note!" The absurdity now begins to show. It should have been apparent from the beginning.

No illusion can be penetrated if its strength is not first understood. An illusion that is not seen is perfectly secure, for there appears to be nothing from which one needs deliverance. If rainbows were so common as to pass unnoticed, we would not need to be told that they are not there. And so with the illusion of selfhood. We have first to see that it does dominate every thought and act before we can hope to be rid of it. Until then we shall simply take it for granted, probably giving it no thought until confronted with what seems to be the fact of its finiteness and mortality.

Consider, then, the force of this egoism, the manner in which it—as though armed with a whip and inexhaustible in its energy—drives one to any folly and stupidity.

A grown man, roller skating with his children and imparting a certain middling grace to the performance, from time to time scans the periphery of the rink for the reward of the eyes of strangers and even of children, following his movements.

Another, visiting a sick friend, a friend who is, perhaps, at the very portal of death, cannot forgo mention of some recent achievement of his own. The perfect understanding

THE ILLUSION OF SELFHOOD

that this could not possibly matter, could not possibly have the slightest significance in these circumstances, does not stay the tongue—the thing has got to be said. At the heart of the story is of course the self, always the central actor.

Another spends his life's energy building a monument to himself—an edifice bearing his name, an institution that will be associated with him, a little empire, something of this sort. It matters not what it is, provided it is ostentatious and its reference to himself is evident. This is so common that it is widely assumed to be a universal need, not subject to question.

The love of this self even extends to its ornaments, which require no excuse at all for thoughtless and vulgar display. "Here am I" then becomes something similarly intoxicating: "Here are things that are mine." And here again of course the crucial reference is not to those things, but to that ego which is imagined to be at their center. Thus are one's children dressed up and displayed, with notices, degrees, stunning connections. It would all be meaningless but for the supposed connection to oneself, the central ego. Exactly the same is often done with pet dogs and of course inanimate things that are considered rare or beautiful, or sometimes, merely expensive, or which can in any way whatever cast a reflection of their worth upon the egos of their possessors. Such things may be utterly trivial, even vulgar; it does not matter, so long as they, like stage lights, can serve to highlight the self which they surround.

Therefore even wise men do not always act wise. The

inner self seems to them real, hardly less so than to the unreflective, and they too dread its obliteration, even in the full understanding that it is indestructible. Like any other illusion, this one can be comprehended but not banished. One can see the total stupidity of another's delight at the admiring glances cast his way for some feat of no significance, while nevertheless one pursues delights of exactly the same nature himself. One can feel shame at the display of his own egoism to a total stranger, perhaps even to a child, and his shame makes him wiser; but it does not necessarily induce him to act less foolishly at the next opportunity, perhaps at the very next moment. "Here am I" thus conditions everything he does right to the end, and indeed, beyond, for its power outlasts even the illusion itself, until his gravestone carries the message, "Here am I!", though more soberly expressed. Yet all there was, even from the beginning, and even from the beginning of time, and to its end—which means, without beginning or end—was the reality of God, or that alone which is not an illusion. It is worth something to understand this, however little that understanding will do in diminishing the illusion of the finite and mortal self dwelling for a while at the very center of creation.

THE FULLNESS OF GOD

It was inevitable that men should stop believing in God, that they should come to regard it as an embarrassment, a social impropriety, an indelicacy, a mark of vulgarity, to talk about God in normal conversation—as it would be embarrassing to find a grown man prattling, with grave countenance, about childhood things like roller skates and tin soldiers.

Men who know God have all treated the giver of life as something too obvious to belabor, something always there and everywhere, something that does not need seeking, does not need metaphysics, certainly something that needs no magic. But then thinkers took it upon themselves to persuade mankind that there is a God, invented abstruse arguments to prove it and, as the ultimate perversity, treated it as a mark of heroism to assert it! A man who can stand up and say, right out loud with a straight face and in the presence of others, that he believes there is a God, is actually taken, especially by himself, to be something quite extraordinary (which in a way he is) and even someone of great strength (which in a strange way he also is). It is as though someone were to say: "I dare you to affirm something so implausible, so impossible, so absurd! You'll be one to stand amid the saints if you can manage that one!"

Many have been taken in by this challenge. Often they seem to be those who lack the most elementary apprehension of God, who walk on the earth but do not feel it, see her numberless forms without recognizing their own kinship, who breathe without living and pursue without loving. Now, grasping for some straw that might save him after all, a probing cane in lieu of eyes to see, such a man tries this one last feat, something that will set him apart from ordinary men: the affirmation of the absurd, now described as an act of faith and declared to be virtuous just because it is so hard.

It really was inevitable that men should stop believing in God and begin to substitute, for what they would like with all their heart to believe, the capacity to lie.

THE PARABLE OF THE BOX

A great and resourceful man wanted to gain ascendance over a vast tribe of uncouth and illiterate men, to which he belonged. He lacked unusual strength and physical stature, or at least was exceeded in these by others, so no hope lay in that direction. As for magic with which to dazzle and befuddle, he was fairly adept at it, but these tricks were communal property, so the outcome of any attempt to gain prestige by this route was highly uncertain. He decided to put his trust in his wits, and in time came up with a scheme both totally simple and devastatingly effective. He fashioned a huge box and tightly sealed within it something he sagaciously discerned to be absolutely essential to life. He gradually got many to believe this, though he forbade anyone to see into the box, declaring that what was in it might leak out if the seals were broken, and he steadfastly refused to describe its contents, other than saying that the life of the race absolutely depended upon it. Instead, he demanded of them faith. He had a temple raised as a permanent repository for The Box, or, strictly speaking, for its precious contents, since no one was supposed to think of The Box itself as holy, though of course all believers soon did. The inventor of this doctrine became of course its high priest and for all practical purposes the tribal king as well, his powers devolving upon chosen successors after his death, and the teaching which centered upon The Box receiving great and subtle elaboration at their hands. The temple, meanwhile, was added to by succeeding generations, was deemed holy first because it housed The Box, but then eventually came to be thought of as holy and thus essential to life in its own right, partly because of its central place in the traditions of the growing nation. By then temples like it stood in every corner of the land, each containing at its center The Box—or rather, a simulacrum, for no one supposed that the content of the original, necessary to life, was divisible or could exist anywhere but in the primordial Box in the original temple.

As the nation matured, gathered an illustrious history

and a refined culture, the legends, traditions and practices associated with The Box were of course kept up, the priesthood maintained and its works supported, and the notion carefully nurtured, at least in the young of each generation, that all would crumble were it not for The Box, that living things would all perish were it not for what was in The Box. The contents were therefore referred to with solemnity, with strange contrived names, usually only under special, hallowed circumstances. All this became a matter of habit. In their worship, in which they engaged regularly though quite infrequently, people often felt greatly edified in declaring their firm belief in the unseen and unfelt contents of The Box, which they had been granted the gift of faith to affirm.

Eventually there arose men of great sophistication and learning who suggested, tentatively at first but more boldly as their numbers grew, that *there was nothing in The Box.* "It is just a huge empty box," they said. And, short of prying it open and peering in, which would have been an abominable desecration, they tested this disquieting idea by weighing The Box, tilting it this way and that, eventually even X-raying it, the justification for all these probings and antics being, they gravely said, that reverence for the holy cannot be incompatible with the love of truth. Everything appeared to point to a sad truth in this new skepticism. Not once did there emerge the slightest trace of anything in The Box; every test seemed to bear out the negative inference of the preceding ones. So in time it came to be generally accepted that there was nothing in The Box, nothing upon which the life of the world depended, and all social, political and intellectual activities were carried on as though this negative but modern and scientific view were correct. Even the priesthood seemed to go along with it, without actually affirming it.

Still, the old forms were kept up, even new temples were from time to time built and furnished with ornate boxes, with much stress laid upon their symbolic significance. It was often declared in the most respectable quarters that such symbolic significance was, in any case, what the founder of this teaching surely had primarily in mind from the start, and that more literal interpretations of his teaching had been nothing but superstitious accretions during the nation's infancy and had no place in the minds of reasonable men and the heirs of scientific culture. It was now generally recognized (though rarely asserted, except by scholars) that the activities associated with the temples and boxes were ceremonial and nothing else, that religion was only an ornament to civilized life and a unifying factor to men, like gentle manners, flags, legends and those other inventions that make life more agreeable and safe. The Box, everyone believed in his heart, was really empty and always had been. There was nothing in it upon which life depended. It was all just a myth.

But the angels, looking upon these mortals who somehow managed to be at once both terrifyingly sagacious and childishly stupid, both laughed and wept to see them draw breath, filling their lungs, and then with their next exhalation declare:

THERE IS NO SUCH THING AS AIR!

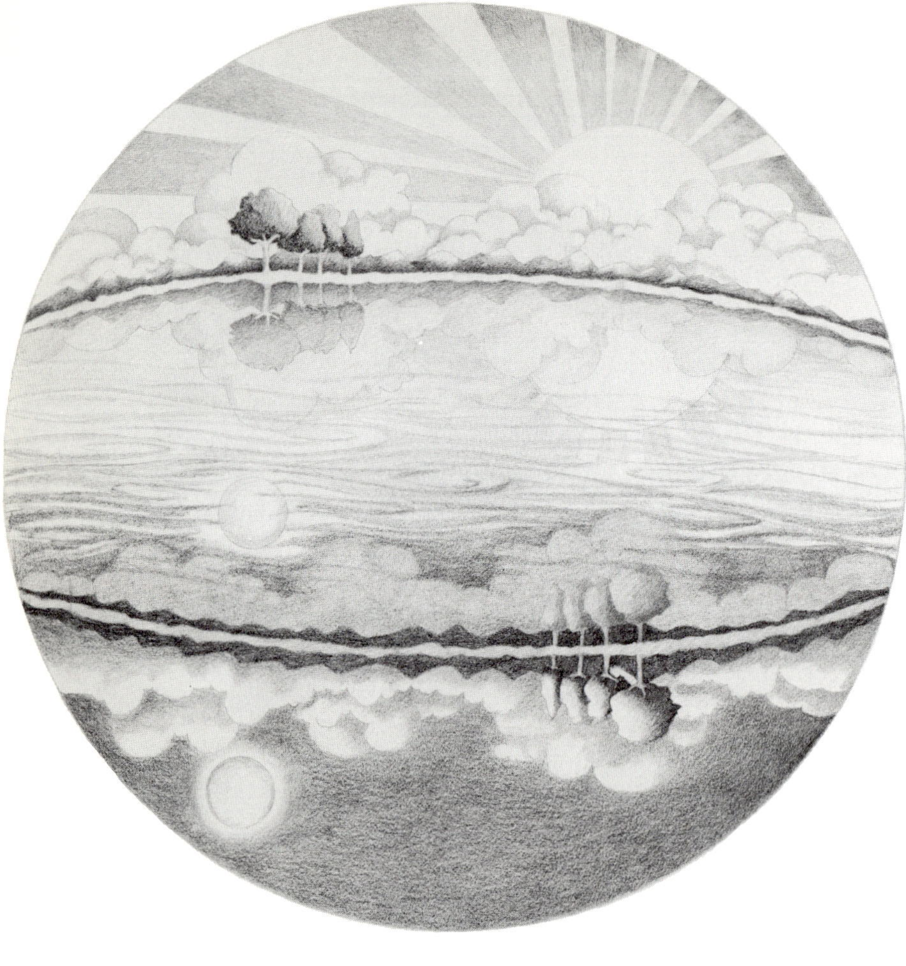

A BEGINNING

True religion is the absolute love of God, and its natural expression is singing, dancing and loving, for nothing provides sweeter rejoicing. False religion is fear, and its expression is reserve, sobriety, rigid moralizing and aloofness. When the love of God is lost, these things are always put in its place, and for a very simple reason: they provide a pathetic kind of security in place of the total security of love.

Religion always begins as something true, for it rests on a vision of the world, on seeing in a certain way, the way that gives life. It can only degenerate into something that is life-depriving; it can never start out that way. So when men think of religion, they usually think of all that is false—musty churches, suggestive of decay; dreary sermons laden with sorrow and guilt; stiff preachers, proud of their wooden virtue; and a kind of moralizing that measures excellence by its paucity of joy.

Do you want to love God? Then don't try. Don't join a thing. Don't go rushing around. Don't talk. Don't, while you are in this frame of mind, study old books; their authors did not find God's love that way. Just live, letting every cell in your body fill with life, bathing in the life that every particle of you shares with all of creation, engulfing this whole within yourself and being engulfed by it. This is the taste of God's love, and once possessed, it will never fail you, never yield to fear or isolation.

Perhaps try this: Sprawl out on your back under a tree and contemplate the leaves; they are all alike and will not distract you. Eventually you will see that they are lovely. You knew this before, but you rarely saw it. Note how the world feels, what it subtly does to you now that you let it, beginning, perhaps, with your toes, your fingers; do not begin with your brain. If a friendly finger or soft lips touch you, don't stir, and you will find these sweet too. They call for no response. If a bird appears above you, study it, but without curiosity; do the same if an insect joins you there; and do the same with a single blade of grass. These are life-giving. The world waited a long time to give them to you. Do not scorn them. Do not make playthings of them. Do not use them. Simply behold them.

Is *that* a religious life? Well, it is a start—but there are millions of others. There is no stunt to it. You don't have to do this and do that. You don't have to torture your brain and deny your body. These are only the ways spoiled children and righteous preachers express their resentment. They have nothing to do with the love of God. It is the seeker who has failed who is stiff, mechanical, moral, self-denying, lifeless. For the love of God, he substitutes these human contrivances and then congratulates himself—not because he has found

A BEGINNING

anything, except ashes, fear and nothingness; but rather, because he has made such a hell of an effort and feels he ought to have some sort of credit for something.

THE MYSTIC

What a fool is the mystic, an impostor or at best a simpleton. He thinks he has a pipeline to God. To find out whether God exists—something about which he has often been curious, something people are always asking—he asks, and down comes the answer: "Yes, George, I'm up here all right. You can tell people so. You have the best proof imaginable—the proof of experience." So he goes out and says so, and if people tell him to prove it, he just talks about his experience. They ought to pay attention to that. If they reject it, then of course they are being irrational. But George isn't being irrational. He has *experienced* God (he says). He is a *mystic*. And mystics have the best reason in the world to believe in God. Therefore, when we run into mystics, we really ought to take their word for it, hadn't we? It is too bad we can't just put *our* question into our end of the pipe and get back the answer. That would be as good as—even better than—picking up the phone to see whether Suzie is home. (Suzie's sister could answer and pretend to be Suzie and fool us. But God would never fool us—if He says He's there, then He jolly well is.) But we can't do that, because we are not

THE MYSTIC

mystics. Mystics are people who can do that—*experience* God, sort of as if they were to run into Him in the street.

That's what we were taught a mystic is. Our professors were all pretty much agreed on this, and they made it so that none of us would ever want to call himself a mystic. An impostor, clearly. Or if not, then at least a simpleton. Irrational. We learned the best way to deal with them. Scorn them. Or laugh and look incredulous. Because *his* getting *his* answers back down the pipeline doesn't prove a thing. He's just making up those answers. When he says he's experienced God, that is because he doesn't know what else to say, because he hasn't got an argument in the world, so he pulls this out and knows we can't refute it. But still it doesn't prove a thing. He just made it up, and he says God gave it to him. Or maybe he really does think God gave it to him. But he was only drunk, maybe neurotic—something like that. What makes him think it was *God?* It really doesn't prove anything.

* * * * *

Well, who was talking about proving anything anyway? Who, indeed, was even talking about asking questions and getting answers?

When the skies lift your sorrows with laughter, the clouds weep for the young robin that fell (the ten billionth one to hatch out and fall); when the fog spreads confusion over the lakes and the meadows so that the birds, bewildered, don't know whether daylight is here yet or not; when the thunder shakes the mountains, then returns to cascade over you and remind you of what you are, and then the warm wind sweeps the fog into the dawn; when the tiny hairs on the body of your beloved beg to be heeded, even loved, caressed in spite of their nothingness; when the impenetrable curtain between you and all of creation is shattered by a fingernail, a whisper, a bead of sweat or a glance that tells the folly that is so inseparable from you; when everything that is ordinary, plentiful, common, is radiant and absorbs for a while your whole mind and soul and feeling; when you are as birthless and as deathless as the setting sun, as minuscule as the ant crawling over your toe and as boundless as the whole earth and sky, being entirely identical with both —you do not need the *word* God, you do not need the artifices of other men to celebrate what is real, you do not need arguments, books or tiresome professors, and it simply does not matter what anyone calls you.

They might even say that you're just some sort of mystic— and think they have said something.

SEDUCTIVE LOVE

The avowal "I love you" expresses not only the idea of love, but just as obviously, that of the self and of another; and the idea that usually overwhelms the others is not, as generally supposed, that of loving, but rather, the idea of the self. It is for this that the love is deeply felt, except rarely, indeed almost miraculously. "I love you" is then, paradoxically, really the expression of love for oneself and nothing else, and is perfectly compatible with nothing more worthy than a grasping or possessive regard for its declared object. The overpowering love of the lover is most likely to be the love for his own ego.

Thus does the declaration of love, which would if genuinely meant be the noblest utterance possible, sometimes become simply a device for coercion and control. This is quite commonly the feeling of parents for their children, and because the passion of loving (in this case, love for oneself) is so unmistakably felt, such persons are apt to believe they really do love their children. And perhaps they do, in a strange way. In such a case the declaration "I love you" is a subtle weapon, deadly effective, intended to weaken another's defenses, render him pliable and subject to one's own will. There is dangled before him something of great but specious beauty, easily given, just as easily withdrawn.

The use of the words by the seducer is very familiar; but seduction is distinguished from loving not by the eroticism of its selfishness and lust, but simply by its selfishness, by its use of an apparent love to attain ends not compatible with loving, whatever those ends might be. The common element in all seduction is therefore simply this: that someone's will is undermined by another's profession of love. Seduction is accordingly aimed at possession, and possession may take many forms. Thus it is not rare for a parent, for instance, literally to seduce his own children, to undermine their wills and thereby bend them to his purposes. The acceptability of those purposes—and even sometimes, perhaps, their nobility—does not modify the basic element of seduction. If a mother manipulates her own children by a profession of love, having quite sincerely their own good as her objective, it is still a seduction, though not one that is entirely base. What is to be stressed is that it is not the love it appears to be; and the concern for another's good does not convert it to true love. It is seductive love.

Love itself cannot possibly be seductive; the very expression is a contradiction. To seek to possess is one thing, to love is another. Hence to avow love with the aim of possessing is one thing, to avow a love that is genuine is another. Each absolutely rules out the other, for the motivations are entirely opposed. It therefore follows that what is possessed and thereby prized, cannot be loved, no matter what this may be; and if all mankind were to unite in calling it love, it would not make it so. Conversely, what is truly loved can in no way be possessed. And this might almost have been expected anyway, for the unification of love abolishes the very distinction between possessor and possessed, and makes it meaningless.

... AND MIND

Being religious is not holding certain metaphysical and speculative opinions; much less is it going through prescribed liturgical motions.

To be religious is to be in a certain state of mind. It is in fact to be perpetually high.

In that state one simply does not doubt—not because he conquers doubt, not because feeling overwhelms doubt, but because doubt, finding no nourishment, does not even appear tentatively to cast even the smallest shadow.

When one's entire insides are filled with the love of God, he understands everything but can say only absurdities. Hearing these, others note that they are absurd—and think they have made a discovery.

"WHEN I WAS A CHILD..."

To be grown-up is to be, or at least appear to be, a kind of monster, a being without insides, something that is presentable, which is to say, mechanical, moving in appropriate ways and adjusting the feelings to these. No one ever actually makes it, for our residual childishness (which is all we can claim of a common humanity) never loses its hold for a moment. It is only concealed, in just the way one tries to conceal blushing or trembling.

It is not clear why this is so, why one should be expected to hide what is our clearest common element and to pretend that something more acceptable has displaced it—something like intelligence, reason, nervelessness, the inability to feel pain or to weep for a mere flower. It is not clear why a man should feel diminished when discovered blushing or trembling either—unless these are, again, signs of that childishness he is supposed to have extinguished. It somehow seems ill-becoming that a big man with hairy arms should be acting like a child—giggling, perhaps, or even sobbing.

Or does it? If not acting like a child, then like *what?* A big man with hairy arms? But what is endearing in *that* image?

To cease to be childish, to replace feeling with reason, tears and laughter with a face that moves in predictable ways, to replace the love of pebbles and dandelions with the eagerness for power and name, to replace the need to be tenderly cared for with a frozen acceptance, to replace the simple delight of one's body, of touches, of smells, of soft caress—to replace these with the kind of mantle meant to shut these things out or at least hide them from view, from the view even, sometimes, of their possessor—all these replacements, the steps toward being grown-up, are only steps toward making dying easier.

To be grown-up is not even to stop crying, for no one can possibly do that and be human. The best one can do is stay the tears, remain presentable. To grow up is, rather, to know, for the first time in your life, what you're crying about.

TRUE LOVE

True love is not the faithful man's constant love for his wife, not the mother's incorruptible devotion to her children, not the patriot's lasting dedication to his homeland, not the believer's undying love of God.

True love is motiveless, groundless, blind, irrational; for as soon as any justification whatever for it appears, it becomes something besides love, and inevitably, something less. There are good *reasons* for one to love his wife, children, homeland and God, in case one does love any of these.

True love is the love you feel for the sticks, stones and grass at your feet.

THE VISIBLE CHURCH

The church is a museum, a repository of relics, quickening nostalgia, but killing belief. If a tyrant had the diabolical wish to destroy the sentiment of religion, he could do no better than place churches and temples everywhere—buildings with strange exteriors and interiors, from which emanate strange yet very human sounds, and in which strange things are said with false voice and sober countenance, and where even the holy is represented as something terrible, something of which one is not worthy.

The very edifice screams: "Do you think you feel religious? Then *look* what you are getting yourself into."

The church reminds us how men once really believed, and we tend to think of them as heroes, as men who rose above being mere men. But they were no heroes. They were children, because for them belief was the easiest thing in the world. They did not with great strength overcome doubt. They believed the obvious. If we kept this in mind, the saints would not seem so awesome.

When one walks into a church, he feels as though he were

walking out of the world. Things are even arranged to give him that feeling. It is like a departure, an abandonment of the real, a taking up of the make-believe. But that is exactly to leave God behind! The church, therefore, cannot always have been this. It cannot always have been dark, musty, foreign and false. Men must once have found it not a symbol of what perhaps is not, but the very culmination of everything there is.

The visible church, then, is a corpse. If a man were to regard the cold remains of his loved one as the reality, pretending to find there the thing he adored, the true being of that which he loves, we would call him sick, mad, deranged —though we might be perversely touched by a hint of heroism in it all, by his somehow managing to carry off such an act and even appearing to be a little convinced himself, like the faithful dog guarding the grave. But certainly the thing to insist upon is this: what he pretends to love is a relic, a reminder, nothing more. That which was loved was real, and he did not need to pretend to love it, it was no feat to love, he needed no special strength for it. He did just simply love, and he couldn't help it.

Such love is possible, for not all of reality is a corpse, nor are the dead its proper symbols. And it is also still possible to believe in the obvious, to find God at your very doorstep. But don't put on a grave face; don't expect praise, as though you were pulling off a feat; don't kid yourself, nor try to kid others. Believing is like loving, and no honest lover makes such an ass of himself.

NATURA NATURANS

The world was not made by God. It is made of God. God is both the creator of all that is real and that very reality. Believing in God is therefore not believing (or trying to believe) in some farfetched metaphysical hypothesis, nor embracing some all-encompassing theological scheme fabricated by this man or that in a bygone age. Metaphysicians have their own ways of talking. So do theologians. But believing in God is neither a philosophical achievement nor an act of faith, whatever that might be, nor any kind of miracle or gift. It is seeing the world in a certain way. Hence those who do not believe are not simply those who have not studied nor thought, but rather those who have not seen. Becoming religious is thus always felt by the converted to be seeing the world for the first time, whatever may be the symbols in which this theophany is expressed. St. Paul knew what this is like, and had his own way of expressing it, a way that now seems rather quaint. St. Augustine knew too. He thought he heard voices, and from that hour he lived in a different world. St. Thomas knew, and declared his achievements until then to be only straw—achievements that not one man in ten million could match. He had seen dimly until then, but now he saw. Gotama saw it, and from then on was called the Buddha, which means not the learned, but the enlightened. This thought is often and most easily and appropriately expressed as a transition from darkness to light. What makes this mode of expression apt of course is that no one sees in the dark, though there is most certainly a reality to be seen.

God indeed creates the world, but in an act of creating that never began and will never cease. He did not make the world in the sense that reality came into being at his wish, command or gesture, as a magician might produce a rabbit from a hat. Reality can neither start nor cease. Neither can God. That which creates, Spinoza's *natura naturans,* and creation, *natura naturata,* are ontologically one and the same. There are not *two* realities.

Is God thus eliminated? Hardly. One might as well say that such a conception of things abolishes nature—as though anything could do that.

NOT TRYING

If one tries hard not to blush, he becomes crimson, and if one tries not to perspire, it will not be long before he is steaming. The penitent, who tries night and day to overcome impure thoughts, who grits his teeth and clenches his fists to drive the devil from his soul, is quickly riddled with a spiritual devastation, while the wide-eyed child who doesn't try anything is as sweet as the sunlight.

Do not say, then, that you believe in God, for the more often you declare your faith, the less it will be felt, and the harder you try to convince yourself, the more you will doubt, until finally you will need to shout even for your own ears to hear.

Do not say, God is real—but try not to.

PLATONIC LOVE

Men imagine that being loved is being profoundly admired, or at least that the one includes the other, that admiring is a step towards loving, or even that these are only degrees of one and the same thing. The pathway to either must therefore be one and the same as the path to the other.

There is perhaps no better example of that inversion of the true order of things that so vitiates all relations of person to person.

We get this partly from traditional religion. We are supposed to love God because he is great. So, love greatness. Despise weakness, failure. Love the strong-hearted, not the broken-hearted. Love the beautiful, not the plain.

But certainly most of this conception of things we derive from childhood, from those things we never seem able to shake off. Be brave and don't cry (and, as you see, you will be loved). Be strong, cut a fine figure, reflect well on your family, look better than the rest (and, as you see, you will be loved).

Love thus becomes a bribe, something never owed, but freely withheld, never freely given, and we become conditioned to believe, right to the day of our death, in most cases, the deepest of falsehoods and the most damning.

What child is more truly loved than the very one that limps? Pride, which is nothing but self-love behind a facade, goes out to the one who achieves—who wins, perhaps, the very things his parents yearned for but never reached—but for what child are their eyes filled with deep and tender, unmistakable love? And when were you truly loved: when you came home victorious or crushed and defeated? When all around looked upon you in awe or in pity? When you were the vanquisher, or the vanquished?

Nor is the proper image of religious love really that of greatness, power, triumph and beauty. Even declaring these to be infinite does not do the least bit of good, because the direction is wrong to begin with. A God described by philosophers and theologians, a God who is *all* this and *all* that, is perhaps frightening, literally awful, to the minute extent that such a being is even credible. But the God that can be loved, and the only one that is so credible as to make doubt impossible, is a Jesus broken and rejected, a Buddha overwhelmed by an ocean of suffering—a God, indeed, who radiates the only thing in men that hints of the divine and the very thing they want most not even to recognize as real.

The divine in men is not what they share with angels, strange beings who were, after all, only invented to fill the immense gap between godlike mighty men and manlike almighty God. (The psalmist was quite right in saying that angels are in the highest degree terrible.) What is divine in men is not their beauty—which is great—not their soaring intellects, not their unique reason, not their justice, not their souls, not the immortality that has so perversely been promised them, not anything at all that they reflect of that almighty which is the idol and invention of theology. What is divine in men is—paradox of paradoxes!—only what they share with the lowliest and most paltry things in creation! This is nothing but suffering and a man's response to it, which does not consist at all in giving it meaning, but in the discovery that its meaninglessness is invincible.

SUNDAY

The pastor wears a somber expression. He is upright, clean-shaven, conventional, stiff. He wears conservative ties.

The pastor always looks grave, solemn—does he ever rejoice inside? Then why does he act ashamed? He seems overwhelmed with the idea that Jesus died. Didn't he ever read the rest of the story? Or did he assume that was just tacked on?

If he really meant "I believe in God," if he meant it even a tiny bit of the way, if he so much as began to mean it, he wouldn't stand there looking as though he were intoning a death sentence, as though he had lost his dearest friend, as though he were approaching a funeral.

What *could* he do, if those words were even partially meant? He could begin whistling. He could bang on drums and tambourines, or if none were around, bang on whatever was at hand. He could throw his head back and shout. He could sing. He could pray—not beseeching, begging things, not self-abasing performances. There are ways of loving without acting like a slave or a dumb beast. Prayers can have the quality of love songs. Faith, hope and love

SUNDAY

need not be confused with doubt, despair and contempt.

But the pastor looks so reserved. When does he do all his singing and dancing? Does he know how to make love? Or is this, too, a standardized, ritual performance? Does he ever go barefoot? Does he ever feel like pulling off all his clothes and dashing across the meadow and into the river?

The bread and wine of life seem to have become for him the crusts and dregs of self-abnegation. The love of God has become an indenture, and he will be released from this galling burden by penances, by buying God off.

Of course even he doesn't believe that, really, but not having anything else much worth believing in, other than the flag and the drivel of politicians (conveniently forgetting the first commandment), he at least pretends to believe this sort of thing. He has the idea that if he acts more or less as though he were in pain, or at least not rejoicing, then he'll be taken seriously, which is better than nothing. Life has for him become not what the Gospels declare at all, but what we read in pagan philosophers—a rehearsal for dying!

What shall we suppose Jesus did after John had baptized him? Did he get dressed in black? Put on an expression of pain? Look overwhelmed with the joylessness of the world? Begin wearing conservative ties?

Or perhaps did he, emerging drenched from the river and reborn, adopt a ridiculous gait, jogging and trucking down the path, whistling, singing, and snapping his fingers?

The Gospels say he was a god. That isn't too hard to believe, if God means anything to you at all. But do not forget—they *first* insist that he was a man.

PHILOSOPHICAL LOVE

It is generally and childishly supposed that loving is the commonest, even the easiest thing in the world, the sort of thing for which there is the least possible need for any philosophy or even any thought. Anyone can love; it is simply a matter of finding the suitable object, finding something or someone capable of evoking that passion that is simply resting, dormant, ready at the moment to make its force felt. And a suitable or appropriate object is of course one of attraction and beauty. Such a thing is not always easy to find. One has to be patient.

The misconception is fatal, because it destroys its victim and is almost invulnerable to correction. Through it one learns that all loving is hypocrisy, a mode of purchase, a mere giving to get; and the very belief tends to confirm itself.

In truth, loving is the hardest thing in the world, and yet, paradoxically, the easiest, and there is nothing more in need of philosophy and thinking. It is exactly that part of loving that is deemed easy which is in fact almost impossible, while what is in fact easy would seem at first to be wildly impossible.

Loving is easy in this double sense, there are *no* obstacles, except those one's own distorted thoughts pose between one's love and its object, and that absolutely *everything* is its suitable object. That, accordingly, which is thought to be its stumbling block, does not exist at all.

But what makes it so hard that numberless men seem never to find it for more than fleeting moments, if at all, is this: That the very beauty of a loved one, the very quality that is thought to be the desired condition of loving, is in fact its impediment. For the beauty of any object, of whatever kind, is a solicitation to exploit, to seduce or at the very least to possess. And to the extent that one seeks to possess or to use, he cannot love. The urge to possess is love for oneself only, and self-love of this kind entirely overwhelms any love one might feel for anything else.

The appropriate object of one's love can be nothing but the world, or indeed, if rightly conceived, nothing but God. Therefore there cannot possibly be any problem of *finding* it. The obstacles to that love consist of nothing but one's own philosophy, that is, one's thoughts, which have almost from birth woven an impenetrable veil between oneself and the world, and which place the whole of reality at a limitless periphery of that circle, of which one is himself the center. But these are the metaphysical creations of thinking. God did not make them. Nature did not erect them. That veil, though virtually impenetrable, is not even in the world to begin with, has no existence at all and is only put there originally for protection; while that circle, of which one is himself the center, is likewise a figment. Its center is everywhere, which means it exists not at all, and that distant periphery is as much in one's own heart as elsewhere. What, however, but philosophy can remove the dust from our eyes and enable us to see these things? And what is harder than philosophy? And what, therefore, is harder than loving, if one is not a philosopher? How else could that which is totally effortless, unimpeded, free and having the most bountiful object that is possible, be the most difficult attainment imaginable?

LOVE AND FULFILLMENT

"Everything that breathes needs to be loved as long as it lives." So said the wife of my philosophy professor long ago, as she sat painting in water colors a large yellow caterpillar she had found in her garden. The words burned themselves into my consciousness and memory.

Why?

I

Is this a mere sentimentalism, a pleasantry, the sort of thing one delights in hearing because there is something sweet and touching about it, even though no one supposes for a minute that it is to be taken seriously? Is it like the flattering little ingratiations one whispers to his lover or the charming things children are taught to say about Jesus and Santa Claus? Is that why it fixed itself in my mind—as an extraordinary and delightful bit of banality?

II

Or is this a specimen of outrageous hyperbole, something one cannot forget because what it says is stretched to every conceivable limit? Is it like saying that God is good—and then for good measure piling on the words "and omniscient and omnipotent," as though goodness were not enough, to make the claim a great big one? The all-encompassing terms are there, all right—"everything" and "as long as it lives." So perhaps the remark has remained lodged with me as a singularly extravagant one.

But I do not think so.

III

Here we are not told to please be kind to the large and little living things we find around us. We are not told, merely, to pet Kitty and not pull his tail, to feed the birds and be nice to baby sister. Those are remonstrances for children. They are hardly worth a philosopher's time.

What has happened then? Has the artist taken an admonition suitable for children and stunned us merely by decking it out as a philosophical profundity? Is it like encountering in our pathway an enormous ant—which is still only an ant just the same?

Or was my oracle merely being pretentious? It is one thing to be painting a picture of a colorful caterpillar. It is something else to treat such things as though they were capable of human responses. A caterpillar, a mouse, a chipmunk, a bird—these are suitable subjects for cute pictures, they are pleasant conversation pieces, sometimes droll, and indeed charming in numberless ways. But who can suppose they can be, like rational men, appropriate objects of love? It is almost as though one were expected to assume a religious attitude towards the whole of nature. How absurd.

Absurd indeed, to the constrained and paltry-spirited who worship in temples no larger than their own bodies!

IV

"Everything that breathes . . ." Your need to be loved does not spring from your incredible brain. The metaphysician has no greater need for it than the infant or fool. If that were not so, then someone could show the *why* of it, as they show or at least try to show the why of all things intellectual. No one has ever done this. It is a need that is profoundly felt, but not seen, not demonstrated, not summoned or banished at the behest of commanding reason. Its source is deeper than reason and thought. It springs from just being, living, wiggling, breathing. This is no unique possession of yours, though you sometimes act as though you thought so. Other things live, wiggle, breathe—and *everything* that breathes needs to be loved.

Needs?

The love you demand of the world—usually without

admitting it, usually bravely pretending you don't—that love, which is also demanded of you by nothing less than the whole of living creation, is no casual thing, no mere ornament to your being which you can lightly forgo. It is not like sensations of pleasure, with which your activities are sometimes veneered but with which you can easily dispense. It does not just improve your complexion, aid your digestion, put a happy smile on your face and make you a bit more agreeable to your fellows. You need it. Without it you die at the center. Without it the stomach still digests, the kidneys work, the bladder empties and fills, but the spirit perishes, you rot within, and the whole of existence becomes a puppetlike motion. If you flee, like a hermit, it is not because you have overcome this requirement, though you may tell yourself so. You have only despaired of fulfilling it, and it is better to be alone than rejected. Or at least it is not quite so bad.

Do not, then, speak of love as a charm, as something that can be popped into the drawer and then produced from time to time when things become tiresome and in need of enlivening. Do not speak of it as a way of talking and behaving, as though it belonged to the category of nice manners, as though it were a way of treating the cat or baby sister or your wife or your children. Everything *needs* to be loved, has got to be loved, absolutely demands to be loved. Do not say less.

". . . as long as it lives."

Not from time to time, when one could use a bit of

bucking up, but from one's very first breath to his last. In this living things are never surfeited; the need does not diminish when it is fulfilled. No claims of morality ever shrieked so loudly, the commands of God Himself were never so binding, nor the dumb pleas of all living things more beseeching.

No one knows why this is so, but the first thing to understand is that it is so, and with that understanding you can indeed step out of your skin, out of your shell, into the boundless temple of the world.

THE ANGELS

Aristotle described the angels—or what eventually came to be thought of as angels—as *separated intelligences,* and he conceived an imposing hierarchy of them. Though he thought of them as intelligences, expressing the prejudice almost essential to philosophy, he had finally to imbue them with desire too, for otherwise, he was afraid, they would never do anything, would just exist passively and be quite meaningless. Indeed, he had finally to imagine these intelligences to be filled with the love of God—for otherwise, he thought, the whole world would stand still!

It is amazing how childish and unfathomably absurd truth sometimes is.

PARADOXES OF PAIN

It is a fond notion, a piece of sentimentalism cherished by childish persons for whom suffering has never been more than a distant threat—a thing read of, seldom seen, never felt—that suffering teaches, ennobles, humanizes, that it lifts the sufferer above animality and enables him to see where others must grope.

Like so much common fiction, this hideous falsehood does have buried in it a truth, and becomes deeply paradoxical the more it becomes understood.

All suffering is an assault upon the spirit. The body does not suffer, except as this is felt within. Pain is unknowable except within one. No unthinking body knows anguish or frustration, the unbearable cold of rejection. To suffer is to suffer within. There is no other way.

Yet it is only so far as suffering does not touch the spirit that it does in fact ennoble, that it enables one for the first time in his life to love beyond himself, that it does transform him from an empty thing to genuine humanity. Indeed, it raises him to the very company of angels, but in the strangest way imaginable, in the last way that could ever occur to one. It raises him to such splendor by imparting to him visible, unconcealable ugliness! Nor is it that the radiance of the sufferer's spirit needs such a framework merely in order to become visible.

I

From childhood I remember an aged woman, grotesquely bent from long past assaults of a nature that is sometimes cruel—things never inquired about, probably never speculated upon. She appeared friendless, isolated, known by name to everyone, but otherwise entirely avoided, as one avoids the unsightly and makes believe it isn't there. Though untrained for it, she was permitted to run a tiny school, a minute frame structure raised from the ground by wood blocks. To this were sent those beyond hope, children from the edge of the world who had never known sweetness, never seen anything in the shacks they were born in except sickness, poverty and rejection; children stupefied, cast out, whose existence was acknowledged but begrudged. Their school was brightly called "The Opportunity Room," and its mistress received a small stipend.

The thing sticks in one's mind, the years leave the image intact, along with other oddities: marble balls at the gate of the graveyard, the artless fountain, the smelly toilets and stained spittoons of the courthouse. But through the mixed ugliness and vulgarity of this setting there shines across all these years an angel spirit whose love outlasts everything men have made, even long after its source is, by most, wholly forgotten.

The philosopher of morality, wanting to put his finger on something real, would speak here of the good that was done, the good that was sought, perhaps even of balances of good over evil, of pleasure over pain. Such stultifying appraisal wholly misses the point. Perhaps no good was really done. No one will ever know, one way or the other.

Then what?

It is the spirit of warmth and light that pushes back an almost invincible cold. And that is all.

Do not ask, "Did any of the children ever go to college?" It would be nice to think so—but it is not crucial.

Do not ask, "Did she find this rewarding?" It would be nice to think so—but we are rendering things trivial, replacing diamonds with glass. When everything is brought down to an understandable level, it is understood—but why must it be? Can it not simply be seen?

II

Yet how paradoxical, that the very cruelty of nature, which breaks and cripples, should by that very means, and that alone, nourish a beauty that seems out of place in the world, as though the beauty of which the world is robbed had been removed to heaven, there overflowing in a love that, just because it is made seemingly impossible, at last becomes unmistakably real.

And it is, again, in just such an unpromising picture that

one finds the meaning of life, strangely devoid of anything we would have thought of as a mark of such meaning. It both is and is not happiness—for it is not what anyone seeks, even if he is enlightened. It both is and is not satisfaction, for its essence is deprivation, and it would be nothing if it were not so. Perceiving this, we begin to concoct the ideas of heaven and reward—but nothing like that is needed. Happiness, satisfaction and rewards are only defilements. What remains is the light of heaven, that all seek, but that, strangely, can be attained only through the shades of hell.

III

But the other side of the paradox, to the truth that lies buried in this revolting doctrine of ennoblement through suffering, is that when the spirit is wounded, then that very suffering that is fondly thought to ennoble turns the soul to cinders, and no beauty or worldly abundance can ever in the slightest restore it. Nothing can, not even if given a lifetime. The possessor of that mangled spirit is forever a stone that can love nothing, an automaton frantically seeking some hint of life's meaning, who surfeits himself with gratifications in the desperate hope of finding that true love that alone can nourish, but forever deprived of even the smallest grain of it, deprived by the impenetrable shell of his own spirit.

The paradoxes proliferate. All suffering is a matter of feeling, internal, a thing of the spirit—and yet, only when suffering is absolutely manifest, but the spirit is spared, is the richness of life discovered. But when suffering is truly internal, and it is the soul itself that yields to it, then, though suffering may be so totally concealed that not even the sufferer must acknowledge it, the whole of his life becomes hopelessly, irreversibly debased. He is left forever incapable of loving a single thing in nature and is cast out of the world, isolated, forsaken—though he may yet cut ever so great a figure there and be the envy of multitudes. His beauty is an appearance, a facade to the thorn to which his soul is reduced.

And the final paradox is that the destroyer, the mutilator of the soul, is not fire, steel blades and chains, not disease and not pitiless nature, not things that crush or drive one mad. These merciless forces are like raindrops when compared to the true destroyer. That against which all protection is unavailing is—paradox of paradoxes—words, gestures, symbols and signs, nothing more. These are the emasculators of the inner life, sometimes even without the victim's knowledge. They are signs that convey rejection, contempt, exclusion, prompting one to the forfeiture of his own true self in his frantic and vain effort to defend himself and his worth against their subtle onslaught, until he drowns helplessly in a sea of nothingness, surviving as a body—an appearance, sometimes as a beautiful and godlike thing, with even the trappings of power—but dead forever within.

IV

When one thinks of the sufferer, one is apt to think of the maimed or impoverished, of one whose suffering can be figured to sense and imagination, suffering that is clear. It never is, however, for all suffering is within, thereby hidden from any onlooker. And in any case these may be the wrong symbols of it, for there is a deeper suffering, that is hidden even from its possessor, suffering that not merely maims, but kills, robbing its possessor even of the power to feel. And it is found, most unmistakably, in the last places one would look for it.

Think of the clown, whose name and face are known over half the globe, a companion of the powerful, heaped with wealth, the object of limitless envy. It is not the first image one would evoke in trying to imagine suffering, but it could nevertheless be the best image of the purest suffering. Or again, contemplate the grasper of wealth, whose power rivals that of nations, the maker and breaker of both rich and poor, the creator of fates, beholden to none, deferred to by all. The pictures could be varied, but will have this common element: That the subject of each tries to revive his dead spirit with what is mistaken for nourishment, since each man has by his own suffering—the suffering imparted only by signs and words—been rendered incapable of an inner life. So long as the clown is laughed at, so long as, machinelike, there keeps returning to him thunderous laughing, applause, ovation—during those moments he can almost feel loved. Though not one creature on earth loves him much, though he is forsaken by nature and by God, perhaps the multitudes notice him, each a little, for a moment, and perhaps it adds up. And so with the powerful, who can command the attention of a nation and be deferred to by a king. It almost resembles the oneness that can be conveyed in a lover's deep and searching look, and can, anyhow, be preferred to this, quite convincingly. But in truth these are the purest sufferers, for their lives have not only been deprived of all meaning by the corrosion and insidiousness of symbols and signs, but finally, of all capacity for it. Their days can be only motions, repetitions of what preceded, and brief illusions.

V

Possibly the way to convey the nature of such suffering and its total pointlessness is by the representation of a dream, a dream that is in substance the final truth the sufferer possesses. As oblivion approaches, and the magic that has always worked now fails—the formula that has never failed now yields no result at all—the sufferer looks out to see, not a sea of radiant, expectant faces, but a multitude of backs, turned to him in the sincerest disdain. Screaming for one final recognition, for the barest acknowledgment of his being, he watches as his vast audience, unhearing, becomes engrossed in the motions of a few flies and bugs.

EVERYTHING ELSE

"I am sort of a combination Quaker-Buddhist," he said, and from his expression one could see he was highly pleased with this description of himself. It apparently seemed appropriate to the image he had of himself and wished to project for others. A Quaker-Buddhist. No narrow sectarianism here. No archaic theology, either. Philosophy, maybe—one can think of Buddhists as a sort of philosophers—but no theology. And philosophy is respectable, at least intellectually, especially if it is a philosophy associated with another culture. Nothing narrow at all, you see. A Quaker-Buddhist. One gets the image: simplicity and incorruptibility, the highest ideals and humanitarianism, good will for all, that sort of thing; and with it, just enough of the mystical to make it rather interesting, even intellectually respectable.

How perfectly absurd! Why should one want to be religious and at the same time so resolutely refuse to be so? It is like a boy dashing naked for the river, with a great shout, to make the delicious plunge, then only gingerly wetting his toe.

A Quaker-Buddhist! But religion is not something you

shop around for, with the idea of selecting what best suits your needs and your purse. One does not go over the cafeteria counter of faiths, selecting from here and there such dishes as appeal, or such articles, utterances and declarations as seem to say—or can be construed or distorted to say—precisely what one already thinks. If one reads books and joins causes and promotes political notions and talks much with "concerned" people, he is bound to acquire certain habits of thought, certain ways of looking at things. And if, seeking to broaden his mind and become more conversant with things, he goes fishing around in the literature of religions and picks out odds and ends that seem more or less to express these very habits of thought and points of view that he already has, he might find such activity engrossing—something like collecting postage stamps, for instance. But if he *then* comes out and says something like, "I am a Quaker-Buddhist," and fancies that he is describing or even labeling *religious belief,* then the whole performance has suddenly become asinine. He is only using beads and baubles to decorate himself, and it is only in degree less hideous than, for instance, converting a temple to a whorehouse, thinking one is thereby vesting whoredom with spirituality.

SEEKERS

I. THE FOOL

The fool did not say that God does not exist, but he might as well have. What he did say, over and over, year in and year out, was that he thought there might be a good argument for the existence of God.

He had every credential of learning. If he was not in the library, then he was likely to be immersed in a book somewhere or going to and fro with one under his arm. His social life was spent largely in philosophical disputation with friends, and almost always, so far as he could influence the direction of the talk, it centered around the question of whether there is any good argument for the existence of God. He studied tirelessly, even though it had long since become clear, or certainly should have, that he was not likely to run across any really new arguments. Still he kept seeking, as though entertaining the hope that perhaps on the very next page would be just that proof he wanted so desperately to find, that argument that would begin with certain observations he was pretty sure were true (premises), then proceed by an illation that satisfied the rules of logic (validity), and finally emerge into the magic word "therefore," followed by the thunderous, awesome declaration: GOD EXISTS. If only he could find that written up someplace. If only someone would invent such an argument and bring it around for him to see. Then his doubts would be put to rest. Then he would believe. And he would not have to feel so dishonest when called upon to intone with everyone else, "I believe in God, creator of . . . ," and so on. If he could just find such an argument, *then* he could say all those words without blinking —and really mean it! Better still, he could not only believe (which is all religion demands), he could *know,* which is a thousand times better, more secure, more respectable—*almost scientific.* For, if the need should arise—either for stilling any residual doubts of his own or for triumphing over other doubtors—he could always just recite that argument, whose premises would be true, whose steps would be valid and whose conclusion (therefore) would follow. You would just have to accept that conclusion, because it would *follow,* can't you see? You would be a downright ignoramus if you did not accept it. It would almost be a mark of intelligence to see that it follows and that one really ought, then, to accept it. In fact one could say one knew it. And that conclusion, do not forget, was GOD EXISTS. What more could you want? That argument would be as good as bumping right into God in the street. Then you would believe, wouldn't you? Or finding Him right there in the library, with identification card and everything. If that happened, then you wouldn't find it hard to say that you jolly well do believe in God. Well now, such an argument would be just as good as that, for it would prove the existence of God.

And of course, for all we know, there might be such an argument. It might turn up on the very next page or in some book we have not read yet. It is every bit worth looking for. Our fool in fact once imagined he had found just that argument in a special and beautifully subtle version of that delightful monkish joke known to students as the "ontological" argument. For a while he went around proclaiming, with head reverently tilted ever so slightly, that he found it to be valid, and he seemed almost to expect his audiences to draw back in stunned amazement that such a discovery had in this age been made and that they were confronted in fact with its very discoverer. But then in time there turned up an ambiguity in this seemingly airtight argument, and it had to be conceded that it perhaps did not *quite* prove that there is a God. Though it came damn close. Maybe we shall still find an argument, he thought, that will actually do it, one that will "go through." It is well worth seeking. Nothing could be *more* worth seeking.

I found him in the library once, his nose buried in a philosophical book, his eyes red from reading, and I said: "Here, friend, on page forty-three of this book I have found an argument of just the kind you seem to be looking for. It proves that God exists. The premises are obviously true. There is nothing at all wrong with the reasoning. And at the bottom of the page is validly drawn the conclusion, that God exists."

SEEKERS

As he leaped for the book, stumbling over his chair in his desperation to lay eyes on that argument, I snatched it away, fled from the building with him in hot pursuit, reached the bridge and flung the book into the river far below, laughing my head off. Not because I had kidded him; I hadn't. There was such an argument in the book, exactly as I had said. Its premises were true all right, the reasoning was faultless, and it did seem to prove what it set out to prove. But I swore I would never give him the name of the book; not from any wish to treat him badly, but the very opposite. It was just because I did love him, in spite of his idiocy, that I hoped he would see the point.

"But I wanted to see the argument *for myself,*" he remonstrated. "It is just what I have been looking for. I am quite religious, and I do most desperately want to believe. Maybe that very argument would have done it. You said it was a good one, but I can hardly just take your word. I wanted to see for myself."

I wonder when he will raise the question: "Whose word was contained in that book? And in terms of whose ideas are the premises true? And by whose reason are the steps deemed valid?"

If someone were to say to him, "Look, there is a God all right. You can believe it. Because I just said so, didn't I?" And if he were to reply, "Why yes, of course!" and then go his way, thinking he had learned something of transcendent importance, then one would think that he ought himself to be able to see that he is a fool.

Why, then, *is* it so hard for him to see it?

II. THE HERO

The heroic seeker knows the folly of trying to prove the existence of God philosophically or any other way. God, he likes to say with a look of sagacity, is not a "metaphysical principle" or "the conclusion of a syllogism." No, God is the object of worship. So that is what one does: worships Him.

At least that's what our hero says. And for sure, he talks about Him enough. And about Jesus, whom he refers to as "Lord." And about the holy days. Even baptism and endless things like that, things we heard our grandparents allude to.

That's all right, but what makes our seeker truly heroic is his totally *unabashed* affirmation. The more incredible a thing is, the more roundly does he affirm it—as though it were the most obvious of commonplaces, or at any rate, obvious to one of true intellect, who can see the truths of religion. The hero is the religious sophisticate. No one would dream of calling him simple-minded. There *are* simple-minded Christians, there are simple-minded people of all sorts; but not this one. And just because he says the very things the simple-minded say—things about Jesus and the Commandments, about God and the Son of God, about the holy days, the Church and all sorts of things one reads and hears simple people repeating—just because he *says* things of that sort and says them every chance he gets, especially in the company of the wise, just because he says what simple folk say, does not mean *he* is simple. As one can easily see, he is a man of intellect. And his *believing* is *affirming,* loudly, confidently, without the least hint of doubt, without the least hint of absurdity. And this is what makes him heroic: the more absurd his utterances, the more boldly are they made. His religion is a challenge; and his mission, to live up to it. Living up to it is proclaiming *everything,* without the least mental reservation. And that *does* take strong will. So we should not deny that he is heroic. Perhaps all men like the role of the hero, the man of strength; here is how he fills it. He has the courage to utter and even sometimes almost to believe, and always to imagine he believes, that these things really *are* true. That what he says is fabulous makes it all the better. That what he asserts is fantastic, so far out to the edge of credulity that his hearer is stunned, makes it the more delicious. Sometimes it takes more courage to *talk* in certain ways than to face danger. Talking in certain ways, in certain religious ways, in the ways simple men talk so easily, requires an absolutely indestructible pride. Facing danger does not. Imagine a man, with an easily shattered pride, being able to larder his conversation with utterances like, "the son of God," exactly as one might discuss the weather. Unless one happens to be very simple, it takes an indestructible confidence in oneself to do that. Indeed, it takes a hero.

III. THE SIMPLE DEVOUT

Just as, however, a scholar can be a fool—a fool's fool, a seeker with the very brain that is guaranteed to murder the religious life—so too, a hero can be an ass; and while there is a certain security in bold pomposity and windbaggery, they murder religion too.

Religion is not *knowing* anything, certainly not knowing philosophical arguments. And religion is not bombast either, certainly not affirming the incredible.

Religion is belief in the obvious by an unfractured spirit and the faithful heart. When one sees it, he does not need to say anything, much less to say the absurd, the fabulous, the incredible. What one knows is both obvious and unsayable. One could say that what one knows is that God exists, and that would be right, but it would certainly mislead. Someone (the fool) would, with sincerity written all over his face, be sure to ask: "How do you *know* that?" and then stand waiting for an answer. And someone (the hero) would be sure to say, with complacency written all over his face, "Of course, of course," as if he knew what you were talking about.

It is not philosophical to be religious, it is not wise, it is not a mark of learning, of sophistication, nor of courage; for nothing demands less of the mind nor less of sheer audacity. Perhaps we can say that being religious is seeing God and creation in a certain way; but be very careful how you say what that way is.

Postscript: "But that way of going about things doesn't prove a thing."

Indeed it doesn't. Go back to your books. Go back to your solemn declarations, your grave countenance, your sober bearing, your fears, your deceptions, your illusions sprung from fear, your lovelessness, your cold reality. I was thinking about God.

MANY AND ONE

Spinoza, combining uncanny originality and insight with the elegant simplicity that graces so many of his notes and corollaries to his abstruse and awesome speculations, invited us to consider a stone which, having been thrown and now moving through the air, suddenly becomes conscious. This is an idea at once hardly worthy of the dullest student and at the same time so clear and beautiful that it takes a Spinoza to create it.

Unaware of the source that originally impelled it, the stone, our philosopher pointed out, would think it was flying, that it was moving as a result of its own original power and perhaps from its own free will.

The example can be varied in all sorts of illustrative ways and serves to uncramp the philosophical mind that is not content to accept that which is merely widely believed.

Suppose a falling raindrop, for example, should suddenly become a conscious being. It might, as Spinoza suggested, rejoice at its power to move itself earthward, not knowing how it had been formed in the clouds nor of the forces determining its motion. But one thing is very clear, and that is

MANY AND ONE

that it would think of itself as a separate being, just as we think of ourselves. It would think: "Here I am, a separate independently existing being amid countless others like myself, and my tenure of existence is precarious and surely brief. Soon I shall be swallowed up by the sea, and then I shall be no more, though others like me will take my place." In this kind of reflection it is important to see how little is true and why the illusion is clung to so tenaciously.

Suppose the clematis bush now spreading itself over the side of my shop—a plant that unfailingly springs up anew every spring and which I picked up as a tiny root years and years ago in a distant place—suppose that bush were to become conscious, perceptive and even crudely philosophical. It would think the obvious, the unassailable: "Here I am, something new in the world and proceeding through the stages of life. I began as a small shoot, now spread myself out, flower, beget others like myself—and then I shall fade, wither, die and be no more! Beneath me are the residues of the dead that went before. I will join these and be replaced by new beings rather like myself, beings which now exist nowhere, but which will take my place when I am nothing, as they are now nothing, waiting to begin their existence."

We suppose it has not seen the absurdity in which those thoughts culminated, the absurdity of that which is not, waiting to begin being, and that which is, now entering oblivion. Instead, overwhelmed and terrified by this beckoning nothingness, our conscious plant now embraces the following idea, solely for consolation: "Perhaps there is a world in which things like me do not arise and pass away, are not born to die, where things do not even undergo any change. This is a realm in which there will exist a changeless, plastic facsimile of myself—and that changeless and plastic thing will be the *true me,* will be the truly living plant that I really am, and this plant will never grow, never decay, never change at all."

Something has gone hideously wrong here, that the real should become the unreal, that the living should aspire to the nature of the dead. What is wrong is not the fabulous character of our first supposition, that a mere plant might become conscious and think things out in this fashion—for this is not more mysterious than that you and I should do so. What is wrong is the way the whole line of thought began—with the idea, "Here I am, a separate being, new to the world, occupying a finite bit of the world's space, a finite bit of its time."

For I, who am a better philosopher than that, can say: Spring has returned, the earth renews itself, its perpetual joys ebb and flow. And thus the lovely plant I picked up, then an insignificant, dirt-encrusted root years and years ago in a remote place, also unfolds itself as it has from the beginning of time, its many forms arising and passing—which is what separates the living from the dead. Nature, God and the self —which is both an illusion and the only thing there is—never begin, never cease.

CARTESIAN FLIMFLAM

It is fantastic that Descartes should have built a metaphysics upon the proposition "I exist," for this expresses at once the most obvious truism and the grandest, most pernicious and persistent illusion to beset men's minds. That is why it enchants men. An illusion, decked out as the obvious, dances before their eyes, and they want simultaneously to embrace it and, deep in their hearts, to banish it forever from their thinking.

Of course I exist. The whole human race exists, life is lived, the world exists, there is a universe, a totality, God. But Descartes, inching along only upon an immovable firmament, never moving the smallest step farther until he felt *certain* he was still on the path, amazingly built his metaphysics on the great illusion, thinking he had hold of a certainty just because the illusion was so overpowering that he could not *doubt* it.

For Descartes had no sooner noted his existence (the self-evident) that he began treating the world as something whose existence was in doubt, whose credentials were specious and possibly forged by the devil, something in any case removed from himself, a foreign land he was going to have to try to allow for, a strange, dead, humiliating, machinelike realm he was oddly destined to inhabit for awhile—something, in short, that is cold, alien and unfriendly.

Yet to his embarrassment his own *body* seemed to be there already, clamoring for recognition. Our metaphysician looked the other way as long as he could, then bravely tried to see whether this might be treated as a figment of a dream—this body; this bulk; this dead, cold extension. He even pretended for a while that for all he knew, that was just what it was! A dream! Perhaps we need not take it into account at all.

Thus, after removing himself from the world, as a self-conscious and embarrassed child might try to separate himself from his silly, chattering parents and pretend he was no part of them, Descartes performed the most audacious sleight of hand in the history of thought by pretending not to know for sure his own body. That one thing that is truly certain—that there is a world, a nature, God, which is just what is meant when I say *I exist*—turns out to be uncertain. That which is most assuredly uncertain, queer, paradoxical—that at the center of this nature there is a little *ego,* looking out upon it as one contemplates a stage of semirealities—becomes at Descartes' hand the basic certainty of all philosophizing.

That evil and omnipotent demon whose trickery so unsettled Descartes' peace of mind appears to have succeeded in playing, not only upon Descartes but upon a considerable part of mankind, a cosmic joke. Descartes was doubly fooled,

CARTESIAN FLIMFLAM

first by the joke, then by his proof that it is really no joke. It is the kind of joke that, like much fiction, still makes one want to cry, just because the pathos is so impossible to banish. But the point of the joke, after all, is to make you laugh.

DE ANIMA

Some philosophers say that each of us has, or indeed *is,* a personal self, ego or soul, related some way or other to his body and to the rest of the world. Just what those relationships are is much debated; but it is considered beyond doubt that there is at the very center of things this self or ego. Such, at least, is the teaching of a long and respectable philosophical tradition. It is said that this personal self came into being at a certain moment in time, and that, alas, it is going to perish at some approaching moment of time, never to exist again in the whole of eternity. Theologians say it arose as a result of God's creating it and that, if certain of God's expectations are lived up to, it can hope to go right on existing forever in some place specially reserved for it.

Other philosophers say that there is no such thing at all, that a man is nothing more than his body and that his ultimate fate, therefore, is simply the fate of his body, which is known to be dust and ashes. This teaching has the advantage of simplicity and seems generally more scientific, but since it is rather depressing, it is not so widely held.

Both schools of thought seem agreed in this, however:

that a man is a finite being, distinct from everything that is not himself; that he came into being at a certain more or less identifiable moment; and that, apart from the hope nourished by religion, he is going to perish at some future moment not yet known.

Both points of view are basically mistaken on that point, though it is not easy to demonstrate this through philosophical arguments. That should be no cause for embarrassment, for philosophers have never proved anything about this, one way or another, anyway. Each imagines that he has, and dismisses those of a contrary opinion as too dense to follow his demonstrations, but in fact all any philosopher has ever done here is to arrange his presuppositions and prejudices in an orderly way, then step back and say, "Behold what I have proved."

Nor is it easy to show in any other way what is wrong here. Proofs seem to accomplish nothing, except to stimulate controversy. Nothing can be counted on, but we might have some luck with

WALTER'S AMOEBIARY: A PHILOSOPHICAL FABLE

Walter had an engrossing interest in microscopy, but this eventually evolved into an interest in microorganisms and, more particularly, amoebae, not merely as subjects of microscopic study, but for their own sakes. That is, he grew fond of them, studied sympathetically their individual traits and personalities, and in time got to the point of spending hours upon hours in their company. Of course he gave them names: Alice, Henry and so on. The choice of the name was in no way guided by the sex of its possessor, for amoebae are not distinguishable by sex, but this did not matter. Walter found it natural and easy to think of Alice as female, for instance, Henry as male, and so on, considering that an amoeba's name was a perfectly reliable guide in determining whether to refer to a given animal as *he* or *she*.

From the many hours he spent with them, Walter eventually came to know his animals with astonishing understanding. He could pick out Alice at once, for example, knew the circumstances of her birth and something of her achievements, frustrations and failures. When any amoeba seemed sluggish or ill, he felt genuine concern, and when one perished, it was for Walter not just the loss of something easily replaced. The amoebae, to be sure, showed little reciprocation for this devotion and in fact exhibited no more fidelity to their owner than does a cat, but this made no difference to Walter.

It was a harmless little hobby until Walter decided to breed the tiny animals, with a view to improving the strain, and this led him almost to the madhouse. Amoebae multiply rather quickly, but Walter's problems did not arise from this. They were instead metaphysical. There were perfectly straightforward questions, the answers to which he needed for his records, and while those answers lay right under his nose, he somehow could not find them. He became more obsessed with metaphysics than with his amoebae. He was beginning to think himself deficient in intellect, but this was unjustified, for, as he eventually discovered, the questions that plagued him were questions that could not arise.

His frustrations arose in the following way. The breeder of any stock needs to know its ancestry. This would at first seem to be utterly simple for the amoeba breeder, for an amoeba has only one parent. Instead, then, of the usual family histories, with their numberless branches and ramifications, which in a few generations baffle all comprehension, the amoeba breeder would need only a simple linear record of successive parents and offspring. The breed would be improved by encouraging those with the desired traits to multiply and by inhibiting the rest. It all seemed utterly simple. There would be no need at all to pair off prospective parents and then hope for the best, meanwhile becoming mired in the complexities of bisexual genetics.

But then arose the first problem. The amoeba reproduces simply by splitting in two. So if Henry thus divides himself, the question arises, which of the two resulting amoebae is really Henry and which is his offspring? Walter at first answered that in what seemed a perfectly straightforward, unarbitrary way. The parent, he thought, would be the larger of the two; and the offspring, the smaller. In fact it was usually quite obvious when he was on hand to witness the birth, for the offspring first appeared as a tiny bud on the parent, gradually grew larger and then split off. There was then no problem.

But then Walter got to wondering: Why do I record the small bud as breaking off from the larger one to become its offspring, instead of thinking of the large bud as breaking away from the smaller one to become *its* offspring? Is identity a mere function of size? How do I know, to begin with, that a small bud appears on the parent amoeba? Perhaps the parent amoeba withdraws into a small bud and leaves behind the larger remains, its offspring; the parent then eventually recovers its original size and resembles its offspring. How would I ever know, in case that actually happened? How do I know it does not happen every time? So perhaps my records are all backwards, exhibiting a total confusion between parents and offspring?

Walter lost many hours and quite a bit of sleep too, pondering this question, until he hit upon a technique whereby he could, he thought, unfailingly identify any one of his animals, once and for all. He would tag them, he decided. So he developed a technique for imprinting minute but indelible colored spots on them, which could be combined in various configurations. With each animal so marked, he could then know for certain just which amoeba was before him, by checking its markings. Being thus able to distinguish any amoeba from any other, he could thereby distinguish it from any offspring, including its own. He found this particularly useful in those cases of an amoeba's reproducing by dividing itself through the middle, resulting in two animals of the same size. Had it not been for the markings, it would have been utterly impossible to tell which was the offspring, which the original. With the marking system, Walter had only to check to see which animal bore the identifying mark. That would be the parent; and the other, the offspring. He particularly rejoiced at having this system when several times he found that the offspring was in fact the larger of the two divisions, for it was in these cases the bud which bore the identifying marks. This of course confirmed his earlier fear that the larger part might sometimes be the bud that breaks off from the smaller original, so that in truth the larger of the two is the offspring and the smaller one is the parent.

This was all fine, and Walter felt entirely secure in the accuracy of his records and pedigrees, until one day a strange thing happened. One of his amoebae gave birth, but retained only half of the identifying marking, passing the other half to its offspring. Walter found himself totally unable to tell which was which. Without knowing which was the parent, his record of lineage, with respect to that particular family of amoebae, had to come to a dead end, to his dismay.

At first he thought he had minimized the chance of this ever happening again, by making the markings so tiny that it would be very unlikely that they would be divided in any fission of their bearers. But then there arose the following question, which suggested to Walter that the entire system of markings might be unreliable. What if, he thought, a parent amoeba, in shedding some and perhaps even most of its substance to give rise to a totally new individual, should at the same time shed its identifying mark, so that the very mark which was supposed to identify the parent should now be sported by its offspring? Would that not throw the records into a confusion which would be metaphysically impossible to clarify?

For quite a while Walter tried to banish this doubt by insisting that, since marks had been introduced as the very criteria of identity, no question could arise of one amoeba's transmitting its marks to another. The amoeba bearing the marks criterially distinctive of Henry, for example, would have to *be* Henry. It is by those very marks, after all, that we pick Henry out in the first place. To speak of another amoeba as having Henry's marks is to speak unintelligibly.

But like so much that passes for incisive philosophical thinking, this was soon seen to be an arbitrary fiction, from the most elementary consideration. For clearly, if one could regard a given animal as that one upon which a certain mark was bestowed, making its identity entirely a function of this, then one could by the same logic regard a given animal as one upon which a certain name is bestowed. Thus, Henry would be whichever animal one called "Henry," and that would be the end of the matter. But surely such a solution to the problem would be worthy only of children and the most dull-witted philosophers. Our common sense tells us that there would be nothing under the sun to prevent one from flushing Henry down a drain and henceforth calling another amoeba by that name. No animal's continuing identity is ensured by a resolution to continue applying its name. But as an animal can shed its name, so also it can shed its markings—and with that obvious reflection Walter found himself back where he had begun, and on the brink of madness.

After such frustrations, Walter finally destroyed all his records, convinced they must be filled with errors. He tried other systems, but with no better luck. He had long since noted, for example, that his different amoebae displayed different personality traits, different preferences and habits, though all these were of course rather simple. When observing his amoebiary he could quite reliably distinguish one from another by these traits of character, and had in fact been partly guided by these observations in bestowing individual names in the first place. So for a time he used distinctive character traits as his guide, deciding which ameoeba was Henry, which Alice, and so on, simply by how they behaved. It was not difficult, once he got to know them sufficiently well. But then one of the amoebae split, and each of the two resulting animals exhibited the character traits of the original to about the same degree. So it was again impossible to tell which was the pre-existing parent and which the offspring just come into being. It was equally impossible to regard both as having been there from the start, and just as impossible to say that each had arisen with the coming into being of the other. In fact it was impossible to say anything that had any sense to it.

If amoebae only had fingers, Walter thought, so that one could make fingerprints. But were not the distinctive marks the equivalent of fingerprints? And they did not do much good. Or if only one could communicate with amoebae at even the most rudimentary level. That would settle any doubts. If there are two similar dogs, for example, and one wants to know which is Rover, one needs only to say "Rover" and see which dog picks up his ears. But then, what if an amoeba named Henry divided into two, and each half responded to the name Henry?

Walter finally gave up the whole enterprise of records, pedigrees and family histories, deciding that any resolution of the problems they presented would be achieved only by metaphysicians. He went back to enjoying his pets for their own sakes, inspired by thoughts of the grandeur of even the lowliest of God's creatures, and he tried to banish metaphysical puzzles from his mind. Some of the old problems did from time to time unsettle his peace and trouble his sleep, but he resisted fairly well any temptation to try solving them.

In time the truth of things did finally dawn on Walter, however; not in the sense that any of his problems were solved, but rather, that he realized there had never been any problems there to begin with. They were all just problems that could never arise in the first place.

This enlightenment began when Walter started receiving instruction in metaphysical thinking. One of the first things he learned was that all men have souls. This is what makes them persons. If they did not have souls, they would be nothing but bodies, in principle no different from amoebae. More complicated, to be sure, but otherwise of the same order of being. Philosophers refer to this inner soul as the *self*. Since it is what thinks, it is also called the *mind*. Amoebae do not think, because they do not have any minds to think with. It is also this soul which gives men their dignity. That is why amoebae have no dignity. They lack the necessary souls. All this was of course very clear, and Walter began seeing everything in a new and much better light.

What was particularly significant for Walter, of course, was that it is on the basis of the inner self that it makes sense to distinguish one person from another in the first place. This distinction has to begin with the distinction between the self and what is not the self, which of course brings us right back again to the soul. When someone refers to *himself,* he is really referring (though he may not realize it) to his self. He as much as says so. That is, he is not referring to his body, which is only a gross physical thing, continuously changing into other things, continuously arising and perishing. He is referring to his *self*. Therefore this must be something that is not physical. It is related somehow or other to the body, no doubt. It possesses and commands the body, for example. Thus when the self commands the arm to rise, the arm does rise, and in a similar way (readily understood in one's own case) it commands the tongue to speak, instructs it in what it should say and so on. It (the self) retains its unalterable identity throughout all the changes transpiring around it in the world at large and particularly in that part of the outside world that the self refers to as its body.

The birth of the body is therefore not the origination of the person, for everyone knows that the body does not spring into being at birth. It existed before then, as part of another body. Indeed, it has always existed, mingled with other things, unlike the self itself. The person begins when there comes into being a brand new self, or what theologians appropriately call the soul, and philosophers, the mind, the ego, or simply the self. Without such minds or souls, there would only be the corporeal realm, where everything is constantly changing, where nothing is ever created or utterly perishes and where all distinctions between things are relative, as they are in the case of amoebae. In the world considered solely as corporeal, there could be no absolute distinctions between one self and another, for in such a world there would be no selves to distinguish. Hence, in such a world there could be no ultimate distinction between me and thee, mine and thine, for there would not even be the most fundamental and precious of all distinctions, that between oneself and everything else.

Walter saw, of course, that such distinctions as these, so obvious to one who has mastered the fundamentals of metaphysics, do not apply at the level of amoebae. Amoebae are not possessed of egos, selves or souls. *That,* Walter perceived, must be why the distinction between parent and offspring was so elusive. It must be a distinction which at that level does not exist. There one finds only life assuming successive forms, wherein nothing is really born and nothing really dies—unlike that which is discovered, through metaphysics, at the higher personal level.

All this enabled Walter to see pretty clearly what had gone wrong with his attempts to keep records of amoeban ancestry.

If his amoebae had possessed souls, as we do, there would have been no difficulty whatsoever. He would only have needed to keep track of souls and to record the relations of the different souls to each other.

Punch line:

"Then," thought Walter, "everything would have been straightforward, perfectly simple and above all, of course, clear."

A SURROGATE OF LOVE

The man who loves not nature, not God, not himself, but loves instead his own ego, really has nothing to love and thus starves. He loves only in order to be loved, and thereby excludes himself irrevocably. Craving love, he makes it impossible to obtain even the smallest drop—for no one can care in the least for a figment, a ghost, a vanishing decrement. Such a man, therefore, failing totally to obtain even one molecule of what he demands, instantly settles for anything, no matter how grotesque or absurd, that can be fixed up to look like the nourishment he yearns for. Frequent mention of his name becomes a source of gratification, and however often it is heard, he is ready to hear it a thousand times more. Bits of the world receive little labels which read "mine," and he spends the greater part of his life scurrying from one thing to another, affixing these impermanent labels, imagining that by this game the diminutive ego within will somehow become greater, will even become an object of envy, which now replaces the love for which he originally reached. But since envy, however multiplied, never adds up to the tiniest particle of the love that nourishes, it must be supplemented with power over others, thus tightening the deception still more. Thus does a father, having finally lost hope of the love of his children, settle for being feared, dressing this up as respect.

What cannot be loved can, with luck, be flattered; or if not that, perhaps envied; or if not even that, then maybe feared. But what can be loved—which is nothing but oneself, life, nature or God—cannot also be any of these at all.

There are many sides to every view, some of them always false. The man who steps forth into the world, filled with the confidence engendered by power and physical beauty, had better take a look to see whether the stunning impression he makes on all sides might not be the effect of his having forgotten his trousers.

THE INDESTRUCTIBLE EGO

I saw a towering monolith at the edge of a graveyard near my long-accustomed path. It served both as grave marker and as pedestal for an enormous, strange, totally incongruous statue of a fireman. I had never noticed it before, in spite of its extraordinary composition, and not one of my friends who sometimes pass there seems to have noticed it to this day. In graveyards one is only aware of numberless stones of all shapes and sizes. One almost never singles them out or even glances that way. Much less does anyone read the names on them, names inscribed at such cost and labor, in clear, deep, straight characters, made everlasting, ineffaceable, to be read and remembered forever by the living. This seems to be the trusted bond of the dead with the living: the inscriptions of names on rocks. In this way do the buried ones try to reach out to us. It seemed to them, before darkness closed over them, to be the only hold they would have left upon the world of movement and light. They made the most of it then. The stone is there, immovable, imperishable. The name is deeply inscribed; merciless elements will not soon obliterate it. Someone might someday read it; it will be there. Someone may utter the sound, note the dates, count the years, instantly forget—but for just a moment there will be a connection, reaching through the years. At least so it will seem. A name will be mumbled—a name once precious to him who lies there, meaningless to the rest of creation. The dates that will be mumbled mark for him the two most significant moments in the whole of time. To us they are numbers, no different from others.

It isn't much, is it? But it is something. Death takes the rest. The whole of time and space and of earth and sky yield to him. He spares nothing—except traces. We can erect these traces, carve them of stone; they will not soon decay. And why not erect them? It is not much of a victory, but it is something. For one who has nothing else, it is something. It may not be worth a single heartbeat, one breath of air, a touch, a lover's searching look—but it is something. And it lasts.

The gravestone I finally noticed drew my attention because of the enormous statue that surmounted it—the huge spreading hat, boots, ax, courage carved into the expression. This statue stands higher than anything else in that part of the graveyard. Small animals climb about on it in summer. In winter the immovable face stares down the blizzards, day and night, from decade to decade.

The inscription is clear, though unwritten: "I lived, and my existence had meaning that the world must not be permitted to pass over or forget. I was a fireman in this town, and do not fail to note, it is *I* who was a fireman."

It is something. As a dust mote is infinite in comparison to a boundless vacuum, this too is not nothing.

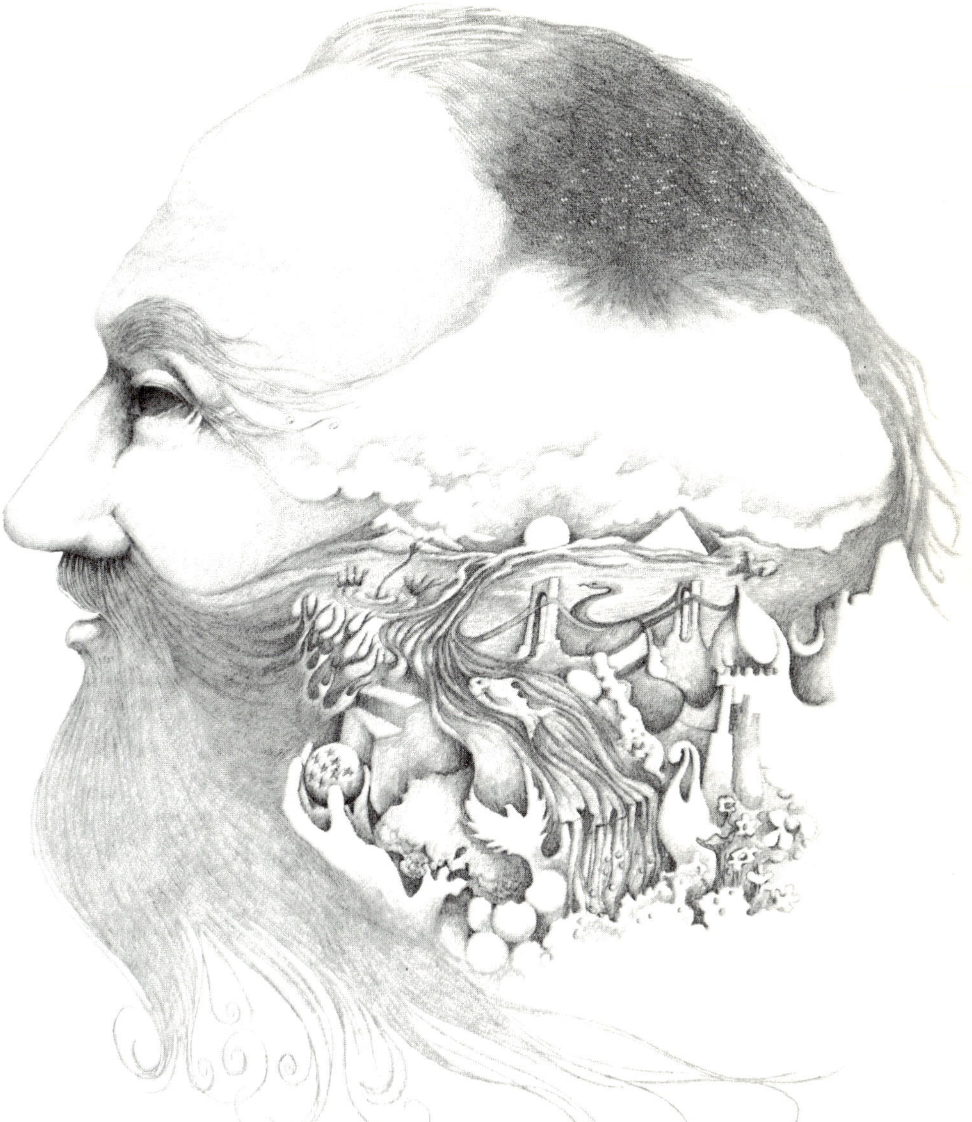

APPEARANCES AND REALITY

Think of a vast river, twisting across a continent, broken at times by waterfalls and rapids, elsewhere broad and gently flowing. Now, disregarding the larger picture, dwell in imagination on one of its least significant aspects, the bubbles that appear from time to time here and there on its surface.

Most of these bubbles vanish almost the moment they appear, while a few cling to existence a bit longer, though none for more than a brief moment. They are terribly perishable, terribly ephemeral.

Now there are two very different ways one can think of this arising and passing away, and these ways mark the division between two distinct metaphysical positions, two ways of conceiving of reality and of human existence. One is filled with meaninglessness and dread, and the other with serenity. Oddly, however, there is no way of showing which is correct. The two metaphysical viewpoints divided the philosophers of antiquity, and they divide thinkers still. All the dialectical machinery, all the wisdom, all the scholarship and science, all the cleverness of man's long history will add not one bit to the balance in weighing these two conceptions. Yet if one fixes his mind on them he can perhaps see which is the fabrication and distortion, the cramp, the entanglement to a peaceful mind, and which is the truth, the scheme that conveys to one a sense similar to that of having come home, tired of pointless struggle, to rest.

There is first of all the viewpoint of the bubbles themselves, if we can for a moment imagine them to be capable of forming a conception of themselves. Such a conception could be expressed thus: Here I am, an individual existent, distinct from others more or less like myself. Like each of these, I came into being at a certain time and at a certain place, and like each of these, I shall utterly perish. The greater river, from which I came, will still go on, perhaps forever, giving rise to ever new existences; but my own tenure of existence is very temporary. I came to the river at one point, as a result of the chance coincidence of numberless chains of events, and I shall inevitably soon depart, never to exist again, the whole river then going on without me, as before, as though I had never been.

That is one way of viewing this arising and passing away. It is realistic and, within the framework that is being presupposed, quite obviously true. A bubble is, within that framework, a separate, discernible existence, having no reality whatever until formed, and ceasing utterly a moment later, without hope of existing again.

But we can also view the whole thing in another way, in a way that is, interestingly, more natural for us who are not bubbles, but detached observers of the changes that unfold before us. For we can say: there does not exist here a plurality of things, the lasting and perhaps everlasting river on the one hand, plus the numberless bubbles that are from time to time superfluously scattered about on it, then haphazardly swept away. There is only the river, which here and there assumes new forms or is modified in this way and that, either briefly or more lastingly. Here it assumes the form of a ripple, there of a waterfall, and numberless other forms in other places. One of the forms is that of bubbles, but these are not things that are added to the river and then taken away; they are nothing but the river itself, as it exists then and there, at that point in time and space. What exists, then, is the vast and everlasting river. It neither comes into being nor ceases. Its bubbles are conceived as separate existences only by a limited imagination. Hence they neither arise nor perish, in any strict sense; we can only say, instead, that the river, the real existence, is ever-changing, presenting the appearance of things being born *de novo* and perishing *in ultimo*. Nor could an individual bubble, if it were a conscious being, truly represent itself as *distinct* from all else or truly make any distinction between itself and others. The only distinctions here are distinctions of points in time and space, not distinctions of real beings. The river, as modified in the form of a bubble here, is one and the same as the river similarly modified there.

The births of the bubbles, as in imagination we watch them arise and float by, are therefore illusions, as well as their perishings; they are neither mortal nor ephemeral, for they have no being of their own either to gain or to lose. The separateness we imagine—indeed, even see—is the separateness of illusion, of failing to see what is in fact before us.

If we could imagine such a bubble forming a conception of itself, or what it would refer to as "I," and of all the others, or what it would refer to as "they," and perhaps cherishing the desire to outlast one or more of them, then *we* could see at once that these conceptions are fictions, mistaking forms for things. But it is when we have seen this and are then seized with the urge to convey our liberating point of view *to others* that we realize, once again, the almost invincible power of the illusion just when we thought we had abolished it.

DOING AND BEING

The meaning of life is the purpose of life, and that is not to *do,* but simply to *be.* While nothing particularly heroic is therefore called for, it is nevertheless not so simple as it looks. It must in fact be extremely difficult, since it is so rare; but the difficulty of it is not that of some extraordinary feat, but rather, the difficulty of seeing things in a true light.

One would have supposed this to be one of life's commonplaces. Obviously every other creature on earth fulfills its purpose, or at least does not stray from it out of confusion and false notions. Yet in fact this seeming commonplace is hardly appreciated at all, and one life after another is made grotesque by its possessor's overwhelming determination to give his life meaning through spectacular deeds, abortive feats that become increasingly desperate with every failure to impart the least particle of meaning. Finally he performs the most absurd stunt of all: he dies. Death in such a context appears as an almost insultingly insignificant imp, which is precisely as it should be, because the whole context was wrong to begin with. How else is anyone going to discover this? If life cannot teach us, then how, otherwise, can death?

DOING AND BEING

No metaphor conveys the absurdity of the life that is conditioned by illusion, but this perhaps hints of it: The acrobat, who has perfected his art through tireless practice and effort over a lifetime, culminates his career with a triumphal performance and then, as he leaves the stage, trips on his shoelace and falls on his face. Someone, on the other hand, who finds his life's meaning in his existence rather than in his deeds is undiminished when all about him has collapsed in decay—like the golden dandelion still opening to the deathless sun, beyond the frosts of late autumn.

EPHEMERAE

I saw the ruins of a stone chimney in such a state of collapse that one would not recognize it as having been a chimney, except at close view. The pile—what was left of it—was very old. Adjoining it one could still discern bits of what had been the foundation of a farmhouse; the indentation in the earth remained and was now filled with weeds and brush, some rusted cans and nameless things. Off to the side was the deteriorated relic of a hand pump, now tipped crazily, its handle gone, as though to challenge belief that it could ever have been a working device.

 One can dwell on such a scene, as his imagination fills in the picture of a once-thriving life, details that must be fairly close to what assuredly was once there The cellar was one time laboriously dug and the foundation planned, measured out, laid with care. Workmen went to bed thinking of what they had accomplished that day, what remained to be done, as gradually the dwelling took shape. A family dwelt there and loved and laughed and sorrowed for things long ago effaced from all memory. Fires warmed the room on fiercely freezing nights, cast their dancing light into the faces of those drawing warmth and life from them. Children fell asleep in their mother's arms, lulled by the crackling flames, the softly-glowing coals. The seasons came and went as children grew, then brought their own children to this scene of their memories. Around the place, now entirely repossessed by nature, were fields, gardens, the livelihood of a farm family, things and projects into which lives were poured. What remains of the touch of man are the collapsed remnant of a chimney, a crude hole, a toppling pump, as if to be the gravestone to human efforts, the hallmark of the death and decay that inevitably, irresistibly overcome all will and purpose. Life recedes; inanimate deterioration gains its hold, then claims all. Nothing escapes it.

What drew me to this spot, though, was a large, neat semicircle of vigorous and brilliantly blooming daffodils, neatly enclosing, in a perfectly ordered pattern, what had ages ago been a chimney.

WEST ORANGE FREE PUBLIC LIBRARY
46 MT. PLEASANT AVENUE
WEST ORANGE, N. J. 07052

735900

191 Taylor, Richard
     With heart and mind.

28